Titles in this series

EDITED AND INTRODUCED BY MARY-ALICE WATERS

D1594180

IN DEFENSE OF SOCIALISM

IN DEFENSE OF SOCIALISM

Four speeches on the 30th anniversary
of the Cuban revolution

by Fidel Castro

Edited by Mary-Alice Waters

PATHFINDER

NEW YORK   LONDON   MONTREAL   SYDNEY

ISBN 978-0-87348-539-5
Library of Congress Catalog Card Number 89-61061
Manufactured in Canada

First edition, 1989
Eleventh printing, 2015

Cover design: Toni Gorton
Cover photo: Gianfranco Gorgoni

Pathfinder
www.pathfinderpress.com
E-mail: pathfinder@pathfinderpress.com

Contents

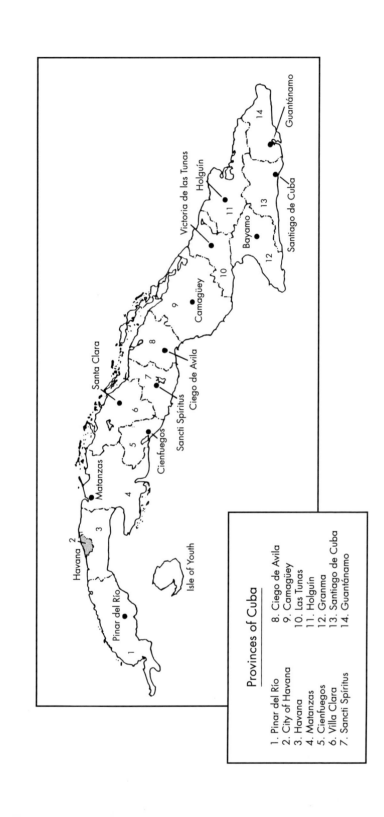

Guantánamo

14

Victoria de las Tunas

Holguín

Santiago de Cuba

11

13

Bayamo

12

Camagüey

10

9

Santa Clara

8

Ciego de Avila

7

Sancti Spíritus

6

Cienfuegos

5

Matanzas

4

Havana 2

3

Pinar del Río

1

Isle of Youth

Provinces of Cuba

1. Pinar del Río
2. City of Havana
3. Havana
4. Matanzas
5. Cienfuegos
6. Villa Clara
7. Sancti Spíritus
8. Ciego de Avila
9. Camagüey
10. Las Tunas
11. Holguín
12. Granma
13. Santiago de Cuba
14. Guantánamo

Introduction

"Socialism is and will continue to be the hope, the only hope, the only road for the peoples, the oppressed, the exploited, the plundered. Socialism is the only alternative! And today, when our enemies want to question it, we must defend it more than ever."

This is the unambiguous and uncompromising conclusion presented by Cuban President Fidel Castro in the four speeches contained in this book. All four were given in the weeks surrounding the thirtieth anniversary of the Cuban revolution, celebrated on January 1, 1989. In them he addresses many issues at the center of world politics today.

"We're now going through a particular moment in the international revolutionary process," Castro told the half million Cuban men and women assembled in Havana on December 5, 1988, in the speech that opens this volume. "As some socialist countries criticize what they have done for many years, as they even deny things that have been affirmed for decades on end," Castro said, it has at the same time become "almost fashionable" in the imperialist countries to proclaim the historical bankruptcy of socialism.

"Imperialism is trying to present socialism as a failure in practice, as a system with no future. And it is extolling to the utmost the alleged advantages of its selfish and repugnant capitalist system."

Defending and improving socialism, Castro argues in these pages, is the task facing Cuba's young generation especially. And, he adds, the challenge is, if anything, greater

9

than what his own generation faced thirty years ago.

Indispensable to meeting this challenge, Castro says, is continuing to train and arm virtually every able-bodied Cuban to defend the revolution so it can develop in peace. As long as the North American imperialist colossus exists, revolutionary Cuba will never be able to lower its guard, Castro emphasized in his December 5, 1988, speech marking that country's Armed Forces Day.

"We are the first socialist country in the Western Hemisphere, the first socialist country in Latin America. . . . We have been the first country to raise aloft the banner of the workers, the peasants, the poor, and to implement their demands and rights. We have been the first country to set the example corresponding to this stage of historical development of the peoples of Latin America. We have upheld those banners for nearly thirty years, and the empire will never forgive us for that. . . .

"We are a symbol, we are the road to rebellion, freedom, and independence," Castro affirmed. And as the history of Washington's aggressions amply confirms, "the empire will never stop trying to crush that symbol, that example, that road, one way or another."

Defending the revolution is not just a question of military strength, however. Today more than ever the defense of socialism is a political battle, both internationally and inside Cuba itself. In these speeches, Castro addresses himself first and foremost to that political battle. He speaks of what has been accomplished in the thirty years since the revolution triumphed, of the unique achievements that have made the socialist revolution in Cuba different from all others. He takes up the mistakes that have been made over the years, and discusses the problems being confronted today through what is known in Cuba as the rectification process. He addresses the youth of Cuba, the generation that has grown up within the revolution, and notes the complex and demanding tasks that the future leaders of Cuba inherit.

The "heroic" days of the revolution are not over, Castro told a mass rally of Cuban young people in the speech that concludes this volume. As long as the revolution is alive and is advancing, those days will never be over. The same kind of collective effort, discipline, energy, and consciousness will always be required in order to be victorious, whether the battle is to defeat South African invasion forces in Angola, or to advance Cuba's economic development by increasing the productive capacities of its working people.

"We face a tremendous historic challenge," Castro told the youth. "Who will win? Who will prevail? The selfish, chaotic, and inhuman capitalist system? Or the more rational and humane socialist system?"

Our battle is the battle to improve, develop, and defend socialism, he told them, "and perhaps the greatest challenge is that this is a battle to improve socialism without resorting to the mechanisms and style of capitalism, without playing at capitalism." That, he insisted, is "what we are trying to do in the process of rectification."

The rectification process, begun in 1986, is the context for much of what is discussed in these pages. As Castro has explained in numerous other speeches and interviews over the last three years, the rectification process is a fundamental political reorientation. It was initiated by the leadership of the Communist Party of Cuba in response to evidence of a growing political demobilization and demoralization among Cuba's working people. These dangerous trends were registered by increasing instances of bureaucratic mismanagement, indifference, abuse, declining productivity and work morale, the growth of corruption and fraud, and frustration over attempts to deal with such problems piecemeal. More and more, Cubans began to see money as the solution to all problems—whether providing incentives to work, or juggling the books of a state enterprise to make it appear efficient and productive.

Castro argued that reactionary policies were being implemented by bureaucrats and technocrats, including by many who thought they were acting as revolutionaries. Despite the rapidly growing number of women either in the work force or who wanted to get a job, for example, construction of day-care centers had virtually ground to a halt. The shortage of adequate housing had reached crisis proportions, especially in Havana. Price-gouging and profiteering in the distribution of food were undermining the alliance between farmers and the working class in the cities, the very foundation of the revolution. The blanket exemption of university students from regular military service was breeding inequality and resentment. Favoritism in hiring and job assignments by plant administrators, as well as the abuse of the bonus system, was widespread, and trade union officials were often complicit. It was common knowledge that materials from state enterprises were diverted to private use with growing frequency. Even in the health care system, a key source of pride for the revolution, there were interminable delays in building new, more adequate facilities, and morale was declining.

As Castro illustrated the problem at a meeting of Communist Party leaders from the city of Havana in November 1987, "those who advocated reactionary ideas within the revolution argued that building a day-care center was a social expense. Social expenses were no good, investing in production was good; as if those who work in the factories were bulls and cows, horses and mares, male and female mules and not human beings, not men and women with their problems, especially women with their problems. . . . Whenever they say no day-care center, you can be sure there is a technocratic, bureaucratic, reactionary concept at work. . . . It didn't enter the technocrat's head that day-care centers were essential to production and the services, and that housing and day boarding schools were also essential to production and the services, and that housing and day boarding schools were also essential to socioeconomic development."[1]

The knowledge that a social layer of relatively privileged bureaucrats, technocrats, and administrators with such attitudes was living in comparative comfort under existing conditions was starting to breed a dangerous alienation and cynicism, especially among sections of Cuba's young people. If not corrected, Castro told the December 1986 session of the Third Congress of the Communist Party of Cuba, the erroneous course the revolutionary leadership was on could eventually lead Cuba not toward socialism and communism, but "to a system worse than capitalism."[2]

In the mid-1970s, Castro recalled at the same congress, Cuba introduced a revamped system of economic management and planning largely copied from those in use in the Soviet Union and Eastern Europe. This helped solve certain problems stemming from previous mistaken policies, he said, but at the same time new and more damaging political errors were introduced. A growing section of the Cuban leadership began to act as if the construction of socialism were basically an administrative task of establishing political and economic mechanisms, such as the new Economic Management and Planning System, or the elected legislative system of People's Power launched during those same years. Somehow, it was believed, socialism would build itself once such institutions and structures were put in place.

But the "construction of socialism and communism," Castro insisted, "is essentially a political task and a revolutionary task, it must be fundamentally the fruit of the development of consciousness and educating people for socialism and communism." Building a new society, based on new property forms, new social relations, and new values cannot be accomplished by administrative measures overseen by a growing (and relatively privileged) bureaucracy. It is the work of creative and productive human beings, women and men who are conscious of what they are doing, communists who are organizing themselves and leading their fellow workers to discover what they are capable of achieving, transforming themselves in the process.

Two political measures have been central to the steps taken during the first three years of the rectification process, and references to both run through these speeches.

First, the Communist Party of Cuba has led a conscious effort to incorporate a new and younger leadership on all levels and in all organizations and institutions. Under the watchword of "renewal or death," the first session of the third party congress in February 1986 made sweeping changes in the composition of its leadership bodies. Forty percent of those elected to the Central Committee and 50 percent of those elected to the Political Bureau were new members.

Just as important were the guidelines under which the renewal took place, with the conscious promotion of more workers, more Afro-Cubans, more women, more internationalist fighters, and more young communists. The result was a more working-class leadership, one closer in composition and experience to that of Cuba's working people today, and one more capable of leading the profoundly revolutionary changes posed by the rectification process.

The leadership renewal begun by the party congress has been pressed forward since that time. It was deepened by the discussions around, and response to, the congress of the Union of Young Communists in 1987. It has been advanced by the demonstrated capacities of the Cuban troops and other internationalist Cuban volunteers in Africa, who in their big majority represent Cuba's young generation. It has taken form in the volunteer youth construction contingents and work brigades that have been part of the rectification process. And it is registered in Castro's January 8, 1989, speech to the youth contained in this volume.

This renewal of leadership is not advancing without political resistance and social friction, however. The relative privileges and conservatism of a social layer are being challenged in Cuba today. The class antagonisms that constitute what Castro has called the "twisted" legacy of centuries of colonialism, imperialism, and capitalist social relations are being confronted more consciously and on a new level. A communist leadership is striving to chart a course that will deepen the revolution by expanding the political involvement of working people, thus bringing changes not only in the consciousness of millions but in social relations themselves. This is the heart of the rectification process.

Political and social conflict is inevitable under these conditions. Rectification is being pursued, however, not by willfully or recklessly tearing the social fabric of Cuba, but by striving to win the broadest possible political unity and support for the domestic and international course set by the leadership of the revolution. The evolution and outcome of this complex process will be influenced by advances and setbacks in revolutionary struggles outside Cuba, as well as by political developments inside the country.

The second measure central to rectification has been relaunching what in Cuba is called the minibrigade movement. The minibrigades are construction brigades composed primarily of men and women who are not professional construction workers but are industrial workers, office workers, and professionals who have volunteered to be released from their regular occupations in order to build badly needed housing, child-care centers, schools, clinics, hospitals, stores, sports facilities, and other needed social projects. These workers are joined by students, housewives, retirees, and tens of thousands of other ordinary Cubans who volunteer to work evenings and weekends after completing their regular jobs. Since 1986 these Cuban working people have already put in millions of hours of volunteer labor. This genuine mass response to the minibrigade movement has made it possible to begin making inroads on problems such as the housing crisis and child-care shortage, which had been worsening at an accelerating pace for more than a decade.

In two years' time, for example, more than 100 child-care centers were built in the city of Havana alone—more than would have been built in a century had the previous policies not been changed.

Similarly with regard to housing, progress is not being made by appealing to people to work longer and harder to make more money to meet their own personal needs while others go without decent shelter. Instead, the shortage is being addressed through mass, revolutionary, working-class action. An organized, collective, voluntary, and disciplined effort is being made to build enough housing to meet everyone's needs. As Castro told a rally on July 26, 1987, the minibrigade movement has the capacity to build a new Havana. It could even build a new London or Paris, he said.

Such a movement is possible, however, only because the Cuban people made a revolution thirty years ago, expropriated capitalist property, and charted a course toward socialism that made them masters of their own resources and of the wealth they produce. Without a nationalized and planned economy and a workers' and farmers' government that implements revolutionary communist policies, such a course would not be realizable.

Alongside the minibrigade movement, the rectification process has spurred the organization of special contingents of skilled construction workers that are taking on major civil engineering projects such as roads and dams. The accomplishments of the minibrigades and special contingents have already brought political changes in attitudes and work norms that are having an impact throughout the society. The spirit and morale of these construction brigades is a product of rising political consciousness, as hundreds of thousands of Cubans discover what they are capable of achieving.

Genuine voluntary work—not a disguised form of obligatory overtime, nor administrative methods devoid of mass revolutionary mobilization—was one of the most notable features of the early years of the Cuban revolution. Volunteer work brigades were an integral part of the revolution. Especially following the introduction of the Economic Management and Planning System in the mid-1970s, however, voluntary work and the minibrigades went into a marked decline.

"The bureaucrat's view, the technocrat's view that voluntary work was neither basic nor essential gained more and more ground," Castro told a mass rally in October 1987 commemorating the twentieth anniversary of the death of Ernesto Che Guevara, the outstanding Argentine-Cuban revolutionary. The attitude developed "that voluntary work was kind of silly, a waste of time, that problems had to be solved with overtime, with more and more overtime, and this while the regular workday was not even being used efficiently."[5]

Guevara, one of the great Marxists of the twentieth century, was among the foremost organizers and proponents of volunteer labor during the early years of the Cuban revolution. He understood its irreplaceable role as a school for developing communist consciousness and revolutionary attitudes toward work. As part of the rectification effort, Guevara's writings on voluntary work, on the economic foundations of the transition to socialism, and on other political and economic questions are being read more seriously and debated in Cuba.

Che has always been honored in Cuba as a leader of great revolutionary initiative and exemplary moral courage. At the same time, however, his political and economic views have often been discounted in academic circles and by economists and administrators educated in the spirit of the Economic

Management and Planning System. Many of them regard Che as somewhat naive, an idealist who expected too much of ordinary working people and didn't understand that they must be motivated primarily by appealing to their material self-interest.

With the communist political reorientation gaining ground in Cuba today, there are more voices defending Che in terms similar to those of Fidel Castro, who stated in his October 1987 speech that without the study and the implementation of Che's ideas, "communism cannot be built."[4] Castro pointed to the scope of the challenge before Cubans in the coming years by reminding them that "no serious attempt" was ever made to put Che's ideas into practice and that, in fact, "there came a time when ideas diametrically opposed to Che's economic thought began to take over."[5]

The political and economic course that Che argued for, like the rectification process today, was based on both a thoroughgoing materialism and a deep confidence in the social capacity—as well as the necessity—of ordinary men and women to transform themselves as they fight to build a new society.

In his speech commemorating the twentieth anniversary of Che's death, Castro introduced a theme that he takes up again in this volume in his speech to the young people. Contrary to what some believe, Castro noted in October 1987, Che was not naive, not an idealist, not out of touch with reality. "But Che believed in man. And if we don't believe in man, if we think that man is an incorrigible little animal, capable of advancing only if you feed him grass or tempt him with a carrot or whip him with a stick—anybody who believes this, anybody convinced of this will never be a revolutionary."[6]

The political perspective expressed in those words is the foundation on which the rectification process rests. It is the basis on which the minibrigades and construction contingents are organized. It underlies the victories won by Cuban internationalist fighters in Africa. It constitutes the challenge before Cuba's young people. It means organizing and leading millions of working people to discover in practice that neither they nor others are incorrigible little animals, but are instead human beings who can collectively transform themselves in the process of accomplishing the seemingly impossible tasks necessary to create a new, more humane world.

"What carrot or what stick motivated the fighters of the Rebel Army who for two years confronted and defeated the army of the [Batista] tyranny?" Castro asked the Cuban youth on January 8, 1989. "What carrot or what stick motivated the 300,000 Cubans who honorably fulfilled their internationalist missions in Angola over the last thirteen years?

"So are we or are we not correct in trusting in people, in their consciousness and spirit of solidarity? Are we or are we not right in feeling people can really do what they set out to do; that people can live in a society that is more humane, more just, more generous, and more based on solidarity than is capitalism, where the law of the jungle prevails? Could a society educated in the selfish ideas of capitalism carry out a single one of these things we've mentioned? That's why our confidence in the future of the revolution is so unshakable."

In the four speeches collected here, Castro frequently refers to Cuba's role in the historic struggle against the South African apartheid regime. In fact, in his speech to the main anniversary rally on January 4, 1989, Castro noted that it would be difficult *not* to link a celebration of thirty years of the Cuban revolution with the peace accords for southwest Africa signed in December 1988.

In March 1988 the combined forces of the Angolan army, Cuban volunteers, and fighters from the South West Africa People's Organisation (SWAPO) dealt a decisive military defeat to South Africa's invading troops at the battle of Cuito

Cuanavale in southern Angola. Castro discusses this battle and its political significance at some length in the first speech in this collection.

Following its defeat in that battle, the apartheid regime was compelled to negotiate the withdrawal of its troops from Angola. In addition, Pretoria agreed for the first time to begin compliance with United Nations Resolution 435, which outlines the steps toward Namibia's independence from South African colonial rule.

As Castro explains in these speeches, however, further steps in the process will not be taken without ongoing struggle, nor is the outcome assured. But the victory registered at Cuito Cuanavale was a historic turning point for all Africa. It was the fruit of thirteen years of collaboration in the battle against South African aggression, a collaboration that has won Cuba the respect and admiration of anti-apartheid forces the world over.

The political stance of Cuba's communist leadership could not be expressed more clearly than in Castro's December 5, 1988, speech. He asserts the simple revolutionary truth that Cuba stands shoulder to shoulder with those confronting the apartheid regime, because "whoever is incapable of fighting for others will never be capable of fighting for himself."

Cuba's solidarity with others around the world fighting for national liberation, for socialism, and for peace is rooted in the convictions expressed so eloquently in these pages. "The question of humanity's survival is a problem that concerns us all; peace is a problem that concerns us all," Castro told the half million Cubans gathered for the Armed Forces Day rally on December 5, 1988. "But even survival and peace have different meanings for different countries. There are two types of survival and two types of peace: survival for the rich and survival for the poor, peace for the rich and peace for the poor." As long as there is injustice and inequality in the world, he stated, that will remain unchanged.

Cuba rejects the imperialist conception of peace, Castro affirmed on January 4, 1989, "whereby peace is understood as being between the big powers, while at the same time they reserve the right to oppress, exploit, threaten, and attack the countries of the Third World. . . .

"We want peace and must strive for it. But we want a peace for all peoples, a peace with rights for all the peoples of the world! Peace with respect, peace with rights, peace with independence, peace with security for all peoples of the world, that's what we must fight for!"

The speeches in this book are eloquent testimony to the vanguard political role of the Cuban revolution and to the communist leadership it is giving to the defense of socialism on a world scale. They deserve to be read and studied by all those who are searching for answers to the great questions facing humanity today.

*

Originally published in English in *Granma Weekly Review*, the translations of these speeches have been revised by Pathfinder for this volume. Other speeches by Fidel Castro that are quoted in this introduction are available in English from Pathfinder.

Mary-Alice Waters
MAY 1, 1989

As long as the empire exists we will never lower our guard

December 5, 1988

Compañeras and compañeros of the Revolutionary Armed Forces and the Territorial Troop Militias;
Fellow citizens of the capital and all of Cuba:

This day has special characteristics. We're not just commemorating the thirty-second anniversary of our glorious

---

This speech was given to a rally of half a million people in Havana's Plaza of the Revolution to commemorate Armed Forces Day, December 2. On that date in 1956 the yacht Granma *landed on Cuban soil, bearing Fidel Castro and eighty-one other freedom fighters to begin the revolutionary war against the U.S.-backed dictatorship of Fulgencio Batista. The 1988 celebration was held three days late owing to a visit to Mexico from which Castro had just returned, where he had attended the presidential inauguration of Carlos Salinas de Gortari.*

Prominent in the audience were men and women of the Cuban armed forces and the Territorial Troop Militia. The militia, made up of 1.5 million workers, farmers, students, and housewives, has become a symbol of Cuba's determination to defend its revolution by arming the people. One additional purpose of the rally was to award Havana the Banner of Defense Readiness.

Revolutionary Armed Forces (although we're doing so three days late for the reasons you all know), but also the fact that our capital is receiving, along with several state agencies, the banner of the highest stage of defense readiness.

Chance also had it that just twenty-four hours ago I attended a rally in the sister republic of Mexico held at the exact spot from which the *Granma* sailed thirty-two years ago as well.[1] [*Applause*]

Today is not simply a day for solemnities; I think it is also a day for reflection.

I think that no revolutionary has the slightest doubt of the need for this effort to strengthen our defense. Why so much sweat, why so much sacrifice, why so many days and endless hours when we deprive ourselves of rest, of study, of healthy leisure in order to do this? I believe this is a point of the utmost importance.

We are a small country—an island, what's more—located many thousands of kilometers away from any potential or real allies; ninety miles away from not just the most powerful imperialist power on earth but also the most high-handed and arrogant one. Or as we have pointed out on other occasions, we are not even ninety miles away but just a few millimeters, a few microns, from a piece of our territory illegally occupied by them.[2]

That empire still is and will continue to be, perhaps for a long time to come, just that: an empire, and a powerful one at that.

We are the first socialist country in the Western Hemisphere, the first socialist country in Latin America, the last one to free itself from Spain, the first one to free itself from U.S. imperialism, [*Applause*] the first one to establish full control over its own wealth, the first one to disobey their orders, the first one to challenge them, the first one to carry out the deepest of revolutions on the basis of new concepts, new ideas, new values.

We have been the first country to raise aloft the banner of the workers, the peasants, the poor, and to implement their demands and rights. We have been the first country to set the example corresponding to this stage of historical development of the peoples of Latin America. We have upheld those banners and that attitude for nearly thirty years, and the empire will never forgive us for that.

But it's not just a question of wounding the empire's pride but also of causing a great injury to its imperial interests. We are a symbol, we are the road to rebellion, freedom, and independence. And the empire will never stop trying to crush that symbol, that example, that road one way or another. As long as the imperial domination of our hemisphere exists, that is and will continue to be their goal.

Even if the day were to come when relations between socialist Cuba and the empire improve formally, that would not stop the empire from trying to crush the Cuban revolution. And they don't hide it; their theoreticians explain it, the defenders of the imperial philosophy explain it. There are some people who say it's better to make certain changes in their policy toward Cuba in order to penetrate it, weaken it, destroy it—peacefully, if possible. Others think that the more belligerence shown toward Cuba the more active and effective Cuba will be in its struggles on the Latin American and world scene.

Therefore, there is something that must be the essence of Cuban revolutionary thought; there is something that must be absolutely clear in the consciousness of our people, who have had the privilege of being the first to travel this road: and it is the awareness that as long as the empire exists we will never be able to lower our guard, to neglect our defense. [Applause]

I say this because some people may wonder if it perhaps wouldn't be better to use all that energy, all that effort, and all those resources in building socialism. And I would answer—anybody could answer—that it would indeed be better to be able to use that money, that energy, and those resources to develop the country. But to do so would be an illusion, a grave illusion, a criminal illusion, because that's the price our people must pay for their revolution, their freedom, their independence, their most sacred rights. That's the price that throughout history many peoples have had to pay for their right to exist and, in our case, not just to exist but to exist for something and by something.

We cannot ignore reality and I don't think our people would ever forgive themselves, nor could they avoid paying an extremely high and fatal price, if someday we ignored that reality. It's not that we're pessimists, we're simply realists; it's not that we're against peace and détente; it's not that we're against peaceful coexistence between different political and socioeconomic systems. It's simply that we're being realistic and we must continue to be. And realism tells us that as long as the empire exists and as long as a dignified people, a revolutionary people, exists on this island, our homeland will be in danger—unless one day we debase ourselves so much or behave in such an unworthy manner as to renounce our independence, our freedom, our most sacred and lofty rights. [*Applause and shouts of "No!" and "Fidel, Fidel!" and "For sure, Fidel, give the Yankees hell!"*]

We view with satisfaction and sincerely support the peace policy of the Soviet Union. In addition, as you know, in our statements over the past few years peace, détente, and disarmament are to us inseparably linked to the possibility of development for a large portion of humanity; to the possibility of overcoming the great economic crisis that now afflicts these peoples of the world, which means billions of human beings; to the possibility of a new international economic order; and to the possibility of guaranteeing a more just future for all these peoples.

The question of humanity's survival is a problem that

concerns us all; peace is a problem that concerns us all. But even survival and peace have different meanings for different countries. There are two types of survival and two types of peace: survival for the rich and survival for the poor, peace for the rich and peace for the poor.

In the world of the rich there's hardly any infant mortality. In the world of the rich there's hardly any malnutrition. In the world of the rich hardly any human beings die from diseases that today's technology, science, and preventive measures can avoid. In the world of the rich there's hardly any illiteracy or the type of illiteracy that afflicts the other nations. In the world of the rich there are hardly any shantytowns. In the world of the rich life expectancy is seventy years or more. In the world of the rich they even occasionally destroy food products needed by billions of people in the world simply to sell what's left at higher prices, to boost prices. In the world of the rich subsidies are granted not just so their agricultural products can compete with those of Third World countries, but they also grant subsidies to the unemployed, and there are many of them, since unemployment is something intrinsic to capitalist societies.

Naturally, when peace is discussed, we can't help thinking about the people who die every day in that Third World I'm talking about.

Thus, historical accounts, books, and political proclamations mention World War I and World War II, the number of people killed and the victims. Concerning World War I, I recall people used to say that close to 20 million people died in it; and that close to 40 million died in World War II. The Hiroshima and Nagasaki atomic bombs are mentioned in books and even now humanity is terrified to think that in just one day 120,000 people died, in just one day or after, and that hundreds of thousands suffered the consequences of radiation following that brutal experiment the Yankees carried out over Japanese cities.

But as we have said on other occasions, every day in the Third World 40,000 children die who could be saved. Every three days—and these are statistics given by the United Nations' agencies—120,000 children die in the Third World who could be saved. Every three days as many children under five die as the number of people killed by one of the bombs dropped on Hiroshima or Nagasaki, just children under five! And those who die later on or who experience the horrible consequences of malnutrition and hunger—which not only shorten life but impair the mental and physical development of tens of millions of people—are the consequence of something worse than the toll from the radioactive fallout over Hiroshima and Nagasaki.

And I'm talking just about children. If we include the adults in those countries where life expectancy is half of that in the rich countries, then as many or more people die each year than those killed in World War I.

But something more could be said: As many human beings die every year in the Third World as a consequence of the colonial plunder of our countries, as a consequence of neocolonialism, as a consequence of unequal terms of trade, as a consequence of poverty, as a consequence of the existence of unjust relations in the world, as a consequence of the imperialist policy, than the number of people killed in World War II.

That's why I say there are two types of survival and two types of peace. As long as injustice prevails in the world, as long as neocolonialist and imperialist oppression exists in the world, as long as plundering exists, there will be two types of survival and two types of peace. In addition, there will be two conceptions of survival and peace: socialist conceptions and imperialist conceptions.

We all know how socialism conceives of peace, but we also know how imperialism can conceive of peace. Imperialism developed its armed forces for world domination;

it has military bases in every corner of the earth, powerful naval and air fleets, millions of soldiers. Imperialism's military conception was designed to impose its order on the world, to impose its peace, like the one called *Pax Romana* in ancient times; its military conception was designed to maintain its domination of the world. That is a reality and we must be realists.

There are no socialist naval or air fleets in the world, nor military bases; there has never existed a socialist conception of world domination.

That's why the news that there might be peace, that there might be reductions of nuclear weapons, that there might be détente between the United States and the Soviet Union does not necessarily mean that there will be peace for us, security for us, for other revolutionary peoples, or simply for the independent countries of the Third World.

For how does the imperialist government of the United States interpret peace, how does the empire interpret peace? It's quite possible, it's almost certain that the way the empire conceives of peace is peace among the powerful, peace with the Soviet Union, and war with the small socialist, revolutionary, progressive, or simply independent countries of the Third World; peace with the powerful countries and open or covert wars, dirty wars as in Nicaragua, or genocidal wars as in El Salvador, or low-intensity conflicts—as they call them—with other countries.

That's why it's so important to ask ourselves what the empire means by détente and what the empire means by peace. We cannot harbor any kind of illusions. That's why I said, and say now, that our people will never be able to lower their guard. [*Applause*]

The question of our defense was never in anyone's hands but our own. [*Applause*] It's very important that we realize this! We were never defended by nuclear missiles. We have nothing to gain or lose in this regard if some missiles of one type or another are dismantled or even if there is universal nuclear disarmament—something which unfortunately does not appear to be so close at hand—since our defense never depended on short-, intermediate-, or long-range missiles.

We once had here on our territory intermediate-range missiles and they were withdrawn from our country long ago.[3] For a long time we haven't had any type of defensive missiles. But if all missiles were to disappear one day, we would be happy for the countries being threatened by those missiles, we would be happy for humanity that lives or survives, for humanity that lives in peace or some other very relative conception of peace. None of this, however, would lessen in the slightest the dangers posed for our homeland in the military field.

The empire will continue to have powerful naval and air fleets, powerful armies in many parts of the world, because so far not a word has been said about the empire reducing its naval or air fleets, its military bases, or its armies in the world. These will continue to threaten the small countries, the Third World countries, with or without nuclear weapons.

However, that does not discourage us. It does not discourage us because we know there are solutions to these dangers. We know that even the small nations are capable of struggling against that powerful empire, and the most recent example, the most unforgettable one, was the example of Vietnam. [*Applause*]

This is the clearest example. But contemporary history has shown that no matter how powerful a country, no matter how sophisticated its weapons, it is incapable of dominating, it is incapable of crushing a people prepared to struggle.

On a smaller scale, for example, we have the Salvadoran people, who for eight years have been resisting a torrent of resources, weapons, and imperial training in the genocidal war being carried out in that country. In El Salvador, in Nicaragua, everywhere, there is one undeniable truth: the peoples who are determined to fight are invincible, invincible! [*Applause*] And even Grenada, as tiny as it is and with a small population—if the revolutionary process there had not committed suicide, even Grenada would have struggled and would have been invincible. [*Applause*] Sooner or later, the imperialists would have had to withdraw, even there, in a 400-square-kilometer country with a little over 100,000 inhabitants.

And our people also learned to defend themselves; they learned a long time ago and defended themselves without vacillation. They defended themselves against imperialism's dirty war. They defended themselves against the mercenary invasion at Playa Girón, and even then there were hundreds of thousands of men and women ready to defend their country.[4] They defended themselves heroically during the October crisis; and when the intermediate-range missiles were withdrawn, our people continued to defend themselves. They continued to apply the principle that the defense of our country is in the hands of our own people. [*Shouts and applause*]

Here absolutely no one was discouraged. Here no one was demoralized even for a minute. Here no one surrendered, like one of you just said. Our people assumed their task just as they have throughout the last thirty years. [*Applause and shouts of "Those who have been born and those who are yet to be should know that we were born to win and not to be defeated!"*]

And when a warmongering and aggressive administration was threatening to wipe us off the map, we carried our conceptions of defending the revolution and the country to their highest expression. Consistent with the principles that led us to victory in the mountains of the Sierra Maestra, in the struggle against the imperialist dirty war in the Escambray mountains and other regions of the country, in the battle against the mercenary attack at Girón, our people and our armed forces, in the face of new dangers, drew up and applied the idea of the war of the entire people.[5] [*Applause*]

It is this conception that makes us unconquerable, that makes us invincible, that makes us act out of deep conviction—a conviction based on reality, experience, and history—that no matter how powerful the empire may be, no matter how sophisticated its weapons, it will never be able to overcome us, to bring us to our knees, to conquer us. Even if our country should be physically occupied, it would never be conquered; the people would never stop fighting and they would never cease to win! [*Applause*]

War of the entire people means that to conquer our territory and occupy our soil, the imperial forces would have to fight against millions of people and would have to pay with hundreds of thousands, even millions of lives for trying to conquer our land, for trying to crush our freedom, our independence, and our revolution, without ever succeeding in doing so.

And this truth is valid not only today; other men at other times in the history of our country perceived this truth. It is not by accident that Antonio Maceo, writing in other times, in another era when there weren't 10 million of us, when we were perhaps a tenth of what we are today, when we had a tenth of the discipline we have today and a hundredth of the weapons we have today, said: "Whoever tries to conquer Cuba will gain nothing but the dust of her blood-soaked soil—if he doesn't perish in the struggle first!"[6] [*Applause and shouts*]

We can add to this marvelous idea, Maceo's extraordinary idea, by saying that whoever tries to conquer Cuba will not even gain the dust of her blood-soaked soil, for he will perish in the struggle! [*Applause*]

No matter how powerful the empire, no matter how sophisticated its technique and weapons, it is not in a position to pay the price of an adventure of this kind. Perhaps it will never be willing to pay it, but we know that no matter how high the price of the sacred principle of defending our country and our revolution, we will always be willing to pay it! [*Applause*]

This is what the concept of the war of the entire people means. This is what the principle means that our people can never make the mistake of lowering our guard. It follows from this that it is necessary to continue investing sweat and resources and making sacrifices to strengthen our defense.

Without defense there can be no homeland, without defense there can be no independence, without defense there can be no freedom, without defense there can be no dignity, without defense there can be no revolution. Defense is something that can never be left in someone else's hands; defense is something a people must entrust only to themselves. [*Applause*]

That's what we have done throughout nearly thirty years of revolution and that's why today's ceremony is so special, this moment when the fighters in our capital, men and women who will have to take up their weapons or keep production and services going in the event of war, are receiving their banner of the highest stage of defense readiness. [*Prolonged applause*]

This is not playing at war, these are not mere ceremonies. There are very serious, very sacred things behind this effort, and the empire cannot fail to understand it. That's why we must never neglect our defense for a single day, for a single minute, for a single second, whatever the cost, whatever the sacrifice. The history of our country reveals what our people are capable of, what the ideas of independence and freedom are capable of, what the idea of the revolution is capable of. I believe that very few have written such eloquent pages of heroism and fighting spirit in such a short period of time.

In its time, the Spanish empire, powerful Spain, failed to recognize or ignored our people's strength. What was Cuba's population in 1868? I don't have the exact figure with me, but I don't think there were many more than a million inhabitants, and the war that started in Yara on October 10 lasted ten years and was waged with indescribable heroism.[7]

It was not the entire people who fought against Spain, it was part of the people. At the time ours was still a slave society; hundreds of thousands of men—men and women but mainly men—were enslaved. They made the sugarcane and coffee plantations produce, primarily in the western part of the country. It is estimated that there were approximately 300,000 slaves.[8]

A handful of patriots started that war, independent peasants and slaves, but in the first ten years the war never reached the west; the western population didn't take part in the struggle and the slaves couldn't be freed. Spain not only had hundreds of thousands of soldiers, it also had the volunteers, who were Spanish citizens living in Cuba, and it unfortunately had part of the Cuban population fighting on its side.

I sincerely believe that one of the most heroic struggles for independence was the one our small population waged against a power that at the time was strong, very strong militarily. The other nations of Latin America fought against Spain simultaneously over a vast territory to liberate themselves. On our small island a part of our nation struggled alone against that foreign power.

It's good to remember this on a day like today because the seed of our present dignity, our present rebelliousness, our present patriotism was planted then, in the struggle of Céspedes, Agramonte, Máximo Gómez, and Maceo, which later became the struggle of Martí and of some of these same patriots who were still alive and of many other leaders and combatants.[9]

After nearly thirty years, when the colonial power had been defeated, the liberation struggle, as we all know, was interrupted by Yankee intervention. It was an intervention accompanied by deceit, hidden motives, and lies; an intervention presented as one to liberate our country. It was an intervention that served to take over Puerto Rico—which is still under the imperial yoke—and to take over other territories. It served to impose the Platt Amendment on us and gave them the right to intervene in our country whenever they saw fit.[10] It served to set up a naval base in one of the best bays of the country, where it still stands. It served to impose neocolonialism on our homeland.

But our people didn't stop struggling against such complex factors in which lies and deceit played no small role. Our workers and peasants struggled against all the injustice that the Yankee intervention brought upon us, that neocolonialism brought upon us, that the policy of manipulating our state brought upon us—the policy of taking over our natural resources; of establishing huge latifundia; of taking our mines, our means of transportation, and our services in usufruct, and of exploiting our country; the policy of contempt for our people.

They even believed they had sufficiently indoctrinated us. They thought we had no choice but to think the way they did, to do whatever they thought we should do. If antisocialism was in fashion, we had to be antisocialist. If anticommunism was in fashion, we had to be more anticommunist than anyone else. If racism was in fashion, we had to be racists. If women's discrimination was in fashion, we had to discriminate against women. If gambling was in fashion, we had to be tops in gambling. If prostitution was in fashion, there had to be more prostitutes in our country than anywhere else. If corruption and plundering the state's finances were in fashion, there had to be more plunder in Cuba than anywhere else. If capitalism, latifundism, and corrupt politics were the fashion, we had to be the biggest capitalists, latifundists, and hack politicians of all.

How they insulted this country, how they underestimated it, how they scorned it! And how far they were from imagining that this country and this people, despite all that indoctrination, despite all that apparent docility and submissiveness, would be capable of doing what they did, of carrying out a revolution, of keeping their flag held high for three decades, of developing the forces they developed! How could they imagine that a mercenary army would be enough to control our country? How could they be so contemptuous of the heroism and intelligence of our nation? How could they be incapable of seeing all the audacity harbored in the soul of our people?

That's why on an occasion like this we must remember our most recent history. We must remember the infinitesimal resources with which we began the struggle in this new stage of our history. We must remember the infinitesimal resources with which the attack on the Moncada garrison was organized, the infinitesimal resources with which the *Granma* expedition was organized,[11] the insignificant number of men with whom the new version of the Liberation Army was founded and with whom the twenty-five-month struggle from the Sierra Maestra was carried out.

A few days ago we commemorated the thirtieth anniversary of one of the most important battles among the many that took place during those months. It seems incredible to think of the small number of men with a minimal quantity of weapons and ammunition with whom it was possible to carry out military actions. It seems like something imaginary or fantastic.

The truth is that our small army, whose founding we commemorate today, was able to destroy an army of 80,000 men, and when the war ended the total number of weapons our Rebel Army possessed was not more than 3,000.

This is a great lesson, a great lesson worthy of being kept in mind now when there are millions of us and we have millions of weapons, when we have tens upon tens of thousands, hundreds of thousands of military cadres of different levels, with solid training; when we have weapons that are incomparably more powerful, modern, and effective.

Therefore, this history makes it easy to understand why there's nothing extraordinary about what our people did to defend themselves, how they crushed the dirty war, how they destroyed the mercenary invasion, how they defied the empire by proclaiming socialism on the very eve of the mercenary landing; [12] how they have resisted and have confronted all risks. And especially on a day like today, we must pay tribute to the heroism, determination, and efficiency with which our people have fulfilled their sacred internationalist missions. [*Applause*]

When hundreds of thousands of men and women organized for the defense of the country are gathered here in the plaza, we can't forget one fact that's really extraordinary, that's a symbol of what our people are, of the degree of consciousness reached, and that is the tens of thousands of internationalist fighters who are thousands upon thousands of kilometers from our soil. [*Applause*] I think that is a good measure of the development of our people's defensive capacity. I think that is a good measure of our people's spirit, courage, and heroism.

It is a really extraordinary fact that when we were threatened here, when the empire spoke of crushing us, when the empire forced us to make an exceptional effort in defense, our country never refrained from fulfilling its international duties. [*Applause*] We did this even though we would have had well-founded reasons to suspend our internationalist missions and recall our forces in view of the threat we faced. We were so confident of our people and their capacity for combat that not even for our defenses here did we withdraw a single internationalist fighter from anywhere. [*Applause*] And not only that. We were able to deal with difficult situations, situations we could call critical, while fulfilling these missions.

Enough has not yet been said, and perhaps this still is not the time to say everything that could be said, but I believe that in the last twelve months, in the last year, our country has written one of the bravest and most extraordinary chapters of internationalism.

It all started less than thirteen months ago when the crisis developed in the People's Republic of Angola. It was a really difficult time, it was a particularly difficult situation for various reasons. We had been fulfilling our internationalist mission in that sister country for about twelve years. During those years in which we maintained our presence in Angola, we were true to our commitments not to participate in the internal strife, since each country must solve its own internal problems. Our presence was to serve as a shield against the South African threat, which is what originated our presence in Angola in 1975, at the request of that country's leadership.

On one occasion we had already driven the South Africans back to the border; that was in 1976. That year we had accumulated a large number of troops that we subsequently started to withdraw. When about half the forces we had accumulated in 1976 had been withdrawn, the intervention of racist and fascist South Africa started up in Angola again.

In the southern part of the country we defended a strategic line established in line with the topography of the terrain and the communications required for defense. This line extended from the sea due east; first it was about 300 kilometers long and then about 700—we would have to determine the exact figure—but it extended eastward from Namibe on the coast to Menongue, in the interior of the country. We were about 250 kilometers from the border with Namibia, and the South Africans operated without ever reaching our lines; they operated in the area between our lines and the border. Their main activity involved waging the dirty war against Angola, arming counterrevolutionary groups in association with the United States.

This situation lasted for years, but during all that time the relationship of forces favored the South Africans. Our forces were sufficient to defend that line but not to prevent South African incursions in part of Angolan territory. As I said, that situation lasted for years, until 1987, when the crisis I mentioned came about.

The crisis stemmed from an offensive organized by the People's Armed Forces for the Liberation of Angola (FAPLA) against UNITA in southeast Angola, very far from the eastern end of our lines.[13] The Cubans were never involved in that offensive. This wasn't the first; there had been another offensive in 1985 from a point now known as Cuito Cuanavale.

Cuito Cuanavale was 200 kilometers east of the last point on the Cuban line, 200 kilometers from Menongue. It was where the 1985 FAPLA offensive against UNITA began toward the southeast. When they had advanced about 150 kilometers in that remote region, the intervention of South African forces came about, very far from our lines, 350 kilometers from the last point in our lines, forcing the FAPLA to fall back.

To tell the truth, we had our own views about those operations, and one of our viewpoints was that these types of offensives could not be undertaken without making allowances for South African intervention. We had very clear, very precise, and very categorical views on the issue.

There were no such offensives in 1986.

Our view was that if the aim was to undertake offensives along these lines inside Angola—which is an undeniable right of the Angolan government—the appropriate conditions had to be brought about to prevent South Africa from intervening. The appropriate conditions had to be brought about to prevent South African intervention! We told those advising such operations that they could not be carried out as long as the conditions were not brought about for preventing South African intervention.

Our views were heeded in 1986, but unfortunately they were not heeded sufficiently in 1987 and events unfolded just as we expected. At a given moment in those remote areas of eastern Angola, when the FAPLA offensive was successfully under way against UNITA, the South Africans again intervened with artillery, tanks, planes, and troops.

But in 1987 they did not limit themselves to intervening to stop the FAPLA. As had happened in 1985, this 1987 intervention occurred north of Mavinga. Mavinga is so far away that not even our fighter planes based in Menongue could reach it. As I was saying, this time the South Africans did not limit themselves to repelling the offensive. Instead they advanced toward Cuito Cuanavale in pursuit of the FAPLA and tried to destroy the largest and best group of Angolan troops. Cuito Cuanavale, as I said, is 200 kilometers east of Menongue, the eastern end of our lines. There the South Africans tried to decide the war against Angola in their and UNITA's favor.

Of course that faraway spot was not the ideal place for large battles since logistics and organizing supplies was very difficult. To get from Menongue to Cuito Cuanavale, you had to cover 200 kilometers through the jungle. In other words, the enemy had selected the field of battle that best suited it.

Once that situation had been created—a situation that in truth developed because our military views were not taken into account, a difficult situation that could prove to be decisive—then everybody asked us to act and try to avoid a disaster there. Everybody asked us to act and expected Cuba to solve the problem.

But actually, as we saw it, the Cuban forces and equipment in Angola were not sufficient to solve the problem.

We didn't have enough men and equipment to defend a line more than 700 kilometers long and, what's more, to advance 200 kilometers eastward through the jungle to deal with the problem. We ran the risk of becoming strong there and weak elsewhere, the risk of falling into a giant trap.

Therefore, from the start we saw the situation clearly. We concluded that although the problem could be solved, it was indispensable to reinforce the troops and apply an appropriate military conception. The principle was that you should not undertake decisive battles on terrain chosen by the enemy; you must wage decisive battles when you choose the terrain and strike the enemy in sensitive and genuinely strategic spots.

The crisis situation developed in mid-November. I had just returned from the Soviet Union where I had attended the festivities surrounding the seventieth anniversary of the October revolution. A few days after I got back, the news from Angola started coming in. The situation had become very critical, the South Africans were on the outskirts of Cuito Cuanavale, the threat was serious and there wasn't a minute to lose.

It was on November 15, 1987, when we met with the general staff of our Revolutionary Armed Forces and made the political and military decision to deal with the situation and take the necessary measures. To have done otherwise would probably have resulted in the annihilation of the best group of Angolan troops, with unforeseeable consequences for the survival of the People's Republic of Angola, as well as a complicated situation for our own forces. Therefore, after careful consideration, our party's leadership made the decision to reinforce the troops and help solve the serious problem.

But it wasn't so simple, it wasn't all so simple. There was a complex political situation. Comrade Gorbachev was to meet with President Reagan in Washington on December 7 to discuss important issues related to world peace.[14] The action could be considered inappropriate. It was the worst possible time for a decision of this kind. The question was, either we make the decision or we face the consequences of letting the South Africans operate with impunity and decide the struggle in Angola militarily.

In all truth, the leadership of our party and the leadership of our Revolutionary Armed Forces never hesitated for even an instant. The correct decision was made on November 15, 1987, to be exact. The first thing we did was to send to Angola the most experienced pilots in our air force, to begin aerial actions from the base at Menongue against the South African forces besieging Cuito Cuanavale. Meanwhile, we selected and began sending from Cuba the combat units and necessary weapons to meet the situation and foil the enemy plans.

The air force had a certain effect, but it wasn't enough. We had to fly in a group of advisers, officers, and cadres to Cuito Cuanavale, plus artillerymen, tank crews, and operators of arms and equipment. About 200 in all were sent in to provide support for the Angolans, chiefly technical and advisory support. But that wasn't enough, and by land we had to send tank, artillery, and armored infantry units 200 kilometers away. We had to safeguard Cuito Cuanavale and prevent the enemy from wiping out the Angolan forces and capturing the town, which was becoming a symbol of resistance and of the success or failure of South Africa.

That is how the battle unfolded—and I've only mentioned part of it. We weren't trying to make it a decisive battle. Next to Cuito Cuanavale, which is a municipal seat, flows the Cuito River. There was a bridge over it and the enemy, using sophisticated methods and pilotless planes, was finally able to make it impassable. So one part of the Angolan forces was on the other side of the river, without the bridge, and the other part was to the west, where the town of Cuito Cuanavale is located.

It was a complex situation but not unsolvable. The enemy advance had to be stopped without giving them the chance to wage a decisive battle there. The enemy had to be stopped; they couldn't be allowed to destroy the group of Angolan troops and capture Cuito Cuanavale. A more detailed explanation will have to await another occasion and different circumstances; perhaps it will be a task for writers and historians to give an explanation of exactly what happened there and how the events unfolded.

The Angolan government had assigned us the responsibility of defending Cuito Cuanavale, and all the necessary measures were taken not only to stop the South Africans but to turn Cuito Cuanavale into a trap, a trap the South African troops ran right into.

In Cuito Cuanavale the South Africans really broke their teeth and it all came about with a minimum of casualties—a minimum of casualties!—for our own forces, the Angolan and Cuban forces.

They were set on carrying out the action and they completely failed. But the Cuban-Angolan strategy wasn't simply to stop the enemy at Cuito Cuanavale, but to gather enough forces and equipment to the west of our lines to advance southward and threaten key positions of the South African forces.

The main idea was to stop them at Cuito Cuanavale and deal them blows from the southwest. Enough troops were gathered together to seriously threaten points of strategic importance for South Africa and strike hard at them on terrain that we, and not the enemy, had chosen. [*Applause*]

Our troops advanced southward from the west, with enough men and equipment to fulfill their mission. It only took a few clashes with their scouting patrols and powerful air strikes at their positions in Calueque for the South Africans to realize the tremendous force they were up against, and this change in the relationship of forces was what paved the way for negotiations. No one should think that they came about by chance.

The United States had been meeting with Angola for some time, presenting themselves as mediators between the Angolans and the South Africans to seek a peaceful solution, and so the years went by. But while these supposed negotiations were taking place with the United States as intermediary, the South Africans had intervened and tried to solve the Angolan situation militarily, and perhaps they would have achieved it if not for the effort our country made.

The fact is that the relationship of forces changed radically. The South Africans suffered a crushing defeat in Cuito Cuanavale and the worst part for them was still to come. The truth is they started to play with fire and they got burned. [*Applause*]

Perhaps never in these more than twelve years had they faced so much danger. When we reached the border of Namibia in 1976 we had men, we had a good number of tanks and cannons, but we had no air force or antiaircraft missiles and we lacked much of the equipment we have today.

I must say that our pilots covered themselves with glory in the battle of Cuito Cuanavale and wrote truly extraordinary pages in history. [*Applause*] A handful of pilots went on hundreds upon hundreds of missions in only a few weeks. They had control of the air with the MIG-23s and we must say they carried out a great feat. That was an important factor.

We not only sent our best pilots to Angola, we also sent our best antiaircraft weapons, a large amount of portable antiaircraft equipment, a good quantity of antiaircraft missile artillery. We reinforced our air power and we sent as many tanks, armored troop carriers, and artillery pieces as were needed.

I mentioned the pilots, but it would also be fair to mention our tank crews' conduct, our artillerymen's conduct, that of our antiaircraft defense personnel, our infantry, our scouts, our sappers. [*Applause*] They organized and helped set up impassable mine fields where the South African tanks were blown up in Cuito Cuanavale. [*Applause*] Success was the result of the coordinated action of the different forces there, in close cooperation with the Angolan troops who really acted with extraordinary heroism and great efficiency in the common effort.

The Angolan 25th Infantry Brigade in particular distinguished itself in the battles waged east of the river. It was a common struggle with common merit and common glory. [*Applause*]

In Cuito Cuanavale the greater part of the troops were Angolan; and in our southward advance, which we also undertook in common, the greater part of the troops were Cuban. [*Applause*]

A truly powerful force was brought together. Air, antiaircraft, and land superiority was ours. We took great care to provide air cover for our troops and so, even when the South African planes vanished from the sky after receiving a few good lessons from our antiaircraft weapons, the troops always advanced and took up their positions with a maximum of antiaircraft support. And our antiaircraft weapons were and still are on maximum alert to prevent surprise attacks. We had thoroughly analyzed the experiences of recent wars and we did not give the enemy a single opportunity, not a single opportunity! [*Applause*]

This was not just because of the measures we took on land—fortifying the field, the antiaircraft weapons, the planes—but we also performed construction feats. In a matter of weeks an airport was built for our fighters, an air base that enabled our planes to advance more than 200 kilometers and seriously threaten key spots of the South African troops. There was no improvisation, no adventures, no carelessness on our part. The enemy realized not just that they were up against very powerful forces but also highly experienced ones.

In this way the conditions were created that made possible the negotiations that have continued and have even progressed over the past few months. A radical change in the political, diplomatic, and military situation came about.

In these negotiations the United States has acted as mediator. You can say "mediator" in quotes, but this doesn't deprive its diplomatic action in these negotiations of a certain positive aspect. I say "mediator" in quotes because they are the allies of UNITA and provide weapons to UNITA; by doing that they act as the allies of South Africa. But at the same time they're interested in seeking a solution to the Namibian problem, seeking some peace formula for the region as a consequence of which the Cuban troops will be withdrawn from Angola.

We know that the United States had some sleepless nights over the kind of boldness whereby a small, blockaded and threatened country like Cuba was capable of carrying out an internationalist mission of this nature. The empire can't conceive of this. They are the only ones in the world who are entitled to have troops everywhere, weapons everywhere, bases everywhere. And so the fact that a small Caribbean country was capable of providing support to a sister African nation is something beyond their parameters, concepts, and norms.

It's clear that this internationalist mission carried out by Cuba had a very big impact on Africa. The African peoples, and even African governments that are not revolutionary but belong rather to the right have viewed with admiration the mission carried out by Cuba in Africa. The African peoples know these are troops allied with them; they know that the only non-African country whose troops were sent to defend an African country against the aggression of racist and fascist South Africa is Cuba. [*Applause*]

All of Africa deeply hates apartheid. All of Africa views apartheid as their greatest enemy, an enemy that despises Africa, attacks Africa, humiliates Africa. It's incredible up to what point the African peoples suffer from apartheid, and this has turned African feelings, the African soul, into an ally of Cuba.

The imperialists can't understand very well the reason for Cuba's broad relations on the international scene, Cuba's prestige on the international scene. But the African peoples, who have been so humiliated by apartheid and racism, have been able to appraise in all its dimensions the noble, generous gesture, the historical dimension, the heroism of our people who were capable not only of defending themselves here from such a powerful enemy but also help the Africans in their struggle against the fascists and racists.

We know what the African peoples think—and this is another problem hanging over U.S. policy. The African peoples have viewed the United States as an ally and friend of apartheid and see it as mainly to blame for apartheid's survival. And South Africa has become an embarrassing friend for the United States. Apartheid has become something that is politically negative for U.S. standing before world public opinion, something that stinks in U.S. policy. It is something that even causes it domestic problems, because there are sectors in the United States that condemn apartheid, repudiate apartheid, criticize apartheid. These include the Black population in the United States, and not just the Black population but the minorities who suffer discrimination in the United States, and not just national minorities but also a large portion of U.S. public opinion.

And so apartheid and its alliance with the U.S. government are becoming an internal political problem, hence the U.S. interest in steering clear of it, of making people stop thinking it is associated with or an ally of apartheid.

Similarly the problem of Namibia, occupied by South

Africa, is a problem that concerns world public opinion as a whole. It concerns the United Nations. Long ago the United Nations ordered the South Africans to leave Namibia and many years ago the UN adopted Resolution 435 on Namibia's independence.[15]

Thus the United States could kill three birds with one stone: distance itself more from apartheid to improve its relations with Africa; make an effort to have UN Resolution 435 applied; and finally, what deprives them of so much sleep, obtain the withdrawal of Cuban troops from Angola. These are the objectives the United States has pursued: improving its international image, improving its image in the eyes of the African peoples, making some advance to place themselves in a more comfortable position before world public opinion, and having the Cuban troops withdraw from Angola.

The truth is that Cuba has no economic interest in Angola or in Africa. Cuba has no strategic interest in Angola or in Africa nor can it, because Cuba is not a big power but a small country. Cuba is in Angola by virtue of internationalist principles, by virtue of its feelings of solidarity, because it is doing its duty of helping other peoples. It is doing its duty of helping the African peoples against apartheid, against racism, against colonialism, against foreign aggression. No other country is more interested than Cuba in bringing its troops back; no one is more interested in this than Cuba. No one benefits more than Cuba, no one is more desirous of bringing the troops back than Cuba.

That's why a political solution that gives Angola guarantees, that opens the road to Namibia's independence, that moves the South African troops away from Angola's border and forces them to remain within their own borders, would be highly positive and highly desirable for us. We would never accept solutions that go against principles or beyond principles and that's why we've been able to remain there for thirteen years already, out of principle, out of loyalty! [*Applause*]

As the history of all these years has shown, no national interest, no danger, no imperialist threat would have made us fall into disloyalty or default on our obligations. I already told you that not even when we were being threatened here did we withdraw a single man from Angola, not a single man! Yet no one is more interested than our country in a solution like the one we've been discussing, and no one derives more benefit than our country. Because with all the energy we're investing in this effort, with all the sweat we're investing in this effort, with all those valuable, mostly young men who are over there, our country would have a terrific force to boost our development plans.

The imperialists sometimes believe it wouldn't suit us to find a solution and to bring our troops back, because there wouldn't be jobs available for them. Jobs is what we have a surplus of here; plans are what we have a surplus of here. Our current plans are very ambitious and the returning troops could make a tremendous contribution to develop the country. In this case our interests and wishes coincide with those of the United States. They seek a different objective than we do, but on the basis of such a solution our troops could return home and boost our current development plans.

I believe this helps explain why the United States has worked with a certain degree of seriousness—I'm not saying 100 percent seriousness. Throughout these negotiations every once in a while they played favorites with South Africa, every once in a while! In other words, they weren't entirely impartial.

But also throughout these months the representatives of the United States were able to verify, on the one hand, the seriousness of Angola and Cuba in these negotiations, for I think that was one of the characteristics of the Angolan and Cuban delegations. Who knows how many prejudices the

U.S. representatives had about our delegation, but they had plenty of time to verify the seriousness and, at the same time, the firmness and the principled policy of Cuba and Angola. Throughout these long months of negotiations we know they were able to appreciate that. In turn, they were able to also appreciate the brazenness, effrontery, lack of seriousness, and cynicism displayed by the South Africans.

They have had many opportunities to observe this in their role as "mediators," mediators with plenty of good relations with South Africa.

The fact that no solution has been signed yet, that no final accord has been reached yet, the United States knows that South Africa—the bad faith, the lack of seriousness of the South African representatives—is to blame.

We've advanced a lot, we've advanced sufficiently. Many concessions were made by both parties as the negotiations progressed in setting up a troop withdrawal schedule. Our position was that if a solution was sought based on guarantees for Angola, on noninterference by South Africa in the internal affairs of Angola and the application of Resolution 435, then upon the disappearance of the causes that led to the presence of the Cuban troops in Angola, both Angola and Cuba would be ready to approve and abide by a scheduled withdrawal of the Cuban troops from Angola.

It was on that basis that the negotiations were carried out. Although we've advanced a lot and were almost nearing the final stage, due to the irregularities and the lack of seriousness of the South Africans we have not yet arrived at the signing of the accord, something that the international community and the government of the United States itself are very interested in.[16] The South Africans' irregularities in these negotiations must have caused the United States many a bitter moment.

The discussion is now virtually centered on one small point and that is the question of withdrawal verification.

Agreement has been reached in almost everything. Right from the beginning, Angola and Cuba were the ones that raised the question of verification. What we said was withdrawal with verification, and verification done by the United Nations. We have started talks with the United Nations and already agreement has practically been reached on the general bases for verification.

The point we raised was that withdrawal should be verified on board each ship or each plane, verifying the departure of the personnel or equipment as they leave.

What did the South Africans seek? To verify the falling back of our troops to the north. We replied that there will be no verification of the falling back of our troops. They practically demanded having their inspectors among our troops and that we give them all the information concerning quantity, composition, etc., of our troops, and we said no, under no circumstances.

In the United Nations we explained to the secretary-general and the UN representatives what verification consisted of—it was our initiative as a token of our good faith and seriousness. But we said that we would not furnish any type of information that might endanger our troops, information on their composition and weapons, which is always a security risk.

The Angolans agreed that once the troops had fallen back there could be on-site verification that no Cuban troops remained.

So practically all that's blocking negotiations at this moment is mere details.

They wanted the four-party agreement to make reference to verification and state that it had to be an acceptable verification. To accept the phrase "acceptable verification" is to entitle South Africa to make negotiations difficult, to start making demands and decide whether or not verification is acceptable. That's for the United Nations and Cuba to verify;

only the United Nations and Cuba can decide whether or not verification is acceptable! [*Applause*]

These are the points now under discussion.

I've said we've done our work very seriously and the United States knows it. We've worked to reach fair accords and we are prepared to strictly abide by the commitments we make. But we haven't accepted the violation of any principle. We haven't accepted any kind of demand or blackmail in these negotiations. We have stood very firmly on that and have acted in close coordination with the Angolans because, naturally, we respect the Angolans' viewpoints, opinions, and interests. If at some point the Angolans ask us to yield on a given point, we would immediately yield. Of course, if there's something that concerns us, like the question of inspecting our troops, it would be up to us to accept it or not, and this sort of thing we will never accept. There are things that are up to us to decide and every decision of ours is made on the basis of principles. [*Applause*]

I'm giving you all these explanations today—and it has taken me a little longer to do it—so that you know, so that you understand, so that you realize the essence of this process that brings us nearer to a solution. Now, if there is no solution, Cuba can't be held responsible.

When we decided to reinforce our troops to confront a critical situation that had arisen, we clearly said we weren't after military victories but were merely confronting a given situation, and that we preferred a political solution. If we had no choice but to strike at the South Africans with all our strength, we were going to strike at them with all our strength, but not because that was what we wanted to do. [*Applause*] We didn't want victories at the expense of sacrificing a single life! We didn't want victories at the expense of shedding a single drop of blood! Sacrificing lives, shedding blood is done only when there's no other choice, and whenever there's a possibility of finding a solution without making those sacrifices, we will prefer it to any other solution. And we said publicly: "We're not after military victories, we prefer a political solution." But the conditions had been created for one thing or the other. That was really what happened.

We have conducted our discussions publicly and with absolute seriousness. We've never revealed a single detail of the negotiations. The South Africans were constantly revealing details of the negotiations. Not even once have we violated the rule calling for discretion throughout these negotiations. Therefore we can now say here so that the whole world can hear it—our people, the people of the United States, the South Africans, the whole world: if there is no solution now, it's not Cuba's responsibility. And if they try to make unacceptable demands, violations of principles, then as far as Cuba is concerned we're prepared to remain in Angola one more year, five more years, ten more years, fifteen more years, or twenty more years! I think this ought to be made known. [*Applause*]

Three hundred thousand Cubans have carried out internationalist missions in Angola. If the number of those holding that honor has to rise to 600,000, then it will rise to 600,000. But sacrifices are not made in vain, commitments are not to be violated, honor is not to be stained.

That's why we want to make our position clear for our adversaries: we want a solution. A solution would benefit no one more than Cuba! We are negotiating with the aim of strictly meeting our obligations. Verification isn't even needed; we proposed it ourselves as a token of good faith. When we sign, whatever we sign we will carry out to the letter. If we commit ourselves to abide by this or that, we will strictly abide by it. That's why I say verification isn't even necessary; it's our offer, our token of good faith.

But even the idea we put forth that the negotiations are good for us, that we want to negotiate, that it benefits no one more than Cuba—if that idea leads anyone to confusion, to think that we're willing to sacrifice principles, that would be a great mistake. What we say publicly for the entire people is that we must be prepared to remain there for whatever time is necessary if there's no solution now! Without firmness there's no true peace! Without firmness not even negotiations are possible! [*Applause*]

This is, in essence, what I wanted to tell you in connection with our internationalist mission in Angola.

A large portion of our leadership's time, of my time, of the Revolutionary Armed Forces' time, was taken up with this problem throughout the year. I already told you it wasn't easy making that decision and, above all, I mentioned the moment when the decision was taken. I already told you in essence that it was on the eve of the Gorbachev-Reagan meeting. There were some who came to believe we were plotting against peace, plotting against détente, given the circumstances under which we felt compelled to send the reinforcements. But given the situation I assure you we couldn't have lost a single day, we couldn't have lost a single minute. One minute lost and it would have been too late.

There are moments when difficult and bitter decisions have to be taken, and when that moment came our party and our armed forces did not hesitate for an instant. I believe that helped prevent a political calamity, a military calamity for Angola, for Africa, and for all progressive forces. I believe that decisively boosted the prospects for peace now present in the region.

I believe that on a day like today tribute should be paid to the efforts made by our troops and by our people. This is a mission we can all feel proud of; it is one more page of glory for our fighting people, our armed forces, born on October 10, 1868, and reborn on December 2, 1956. [*Applause*]

There are some who have even dared question the internationalist spirit and heroism of our people, who have criticized it. This is the Yankees' hope: that anti-internationalist currents would arise among our people to weaken us. As we have said before, being internationalists is paying our debt to humanity. [*Applause*] Whoever is incapable of fighting for others will never be capable of fighting for himself. [*Applause*] And the heroism shown by our forces, by our people in other lands, faraway lands, must also serve to let the imperialists know what awaits them if one day they force us to fight on this land here. [*Applause and shouts*]

Now, one last reflection. On a day like today we must be conscious that the battle against the empire is waged not only in the military field, it is waged not only weapons in hand. It is also waged in the ideological field, it is also waged in the field of consciousness.

I was telling you when I began this speech that as long as the empire exists it will never stop trying to destroy our revolution by any means: military means or ideological means; either by military means or by trying to destroy our revolutionary consciousness.

That's why in speaking of defense we must never forget that we must know how to defend ourselves in both fields; in the military field and in the ideological field. We must never allow our revolutionary ideology to weaken! We must never allow our revolutionary consciousness to weaken! [*Applause*] The enemy never stops working in that field, in the ideological battle, in its campaigns against our country abroad and in its campaigns against the revolution inside the country. It's not for nothing that it invests as many resources as possible to soften up our people, to present an idyllic image of its consumer society. If it can't break us, then it tries to soften us up, to weaken us politically, to confuse us, and there are people who let themselves be confused; it tries to weaken us, and there are people who let themselves be weakened.

We're now going through a particular moment in the international revolutionary process. As some socialist countries criticize what they have done for many years, as they even deny things that have been affirmed for decades on end—and we respect everyone's right to criticize what they want to criticize and to deny what they want to deny—we take into account that imperialism is trying to make the most of the situation, to gain the best advantage. Imperialism is trying to present socialism as a failure in practice, as a system with no future. And it is extolling to the utmost the alleged advantages of its selfish and repugnant capitalist system.

Never before have the imperialists applauded so much. Never before have they tried to praise their system so much. This is an interesting lesson for revolutionaries. It is undeniable proof of the long ideological struggle that lies ahead for socialism and Marxism-Leninism. [*Applause*]

In imperialist societies today, it is almost fashionable to question our objectives, to question our principles. Today more than ever we must be firm partisans of socialism and Marxism-Leninism. [*Applause*] Today more than ever we must demonstrate our confidence and our faith.

It was Marxism-Leninism and the socialist idea above all that led us to where we are now, that made possible this miracle of making our people what they are today and representing what we represent. Marxism-Leninism is what enlightened us, what made us see clearly. It was Marxism-Leninism, the correct interpretation of our reality, that made victory possible. And it was the consistent application of Marxist-Leninist principles that gave our struggle content, that gave our struggle its great historical social objectives.

It was Marxism-Leninism that gave meaning to the *Granma*. And what meaning would the *Granma* have had without what we have today? What meaning would our struggle at the Moncada garrison or our departure from Mexico or the landing in Cuba or the struggle in the mountains or our victory on January 1 have had? Or our victory over the dirty war, the victory at Girón, the proclamation of socialism—what meaning would there be to the fact that our country is what it is today, the fact that it is first in the world in many things: first in education, first in health care, first in social security, first in employment, one of the first in food, which is proved by the fact that there are no undernourished people in our country. [*Applause*]

The fact that our country, blockaded by the empire for thirty years, has achieved the social and material successes that Cuba has is thanks to Marxism-Leninism and thanks to socialism! [*Prolonged applause*] Without it we would be nothing. Without it there would never have been an October revolution. Without it the colonized countries would have never liberated themselves. Without it there would have been no revolutions in Latin America. Without it there would never have been a socialist revolution in Cuba.

Socialism is and will continue to be the hope, the only hope, the only road for the peoples, the oppressed, the exploited, the plundered. Socialism is the only alternative! And today, when our enemies want to question it, we must defend it more than ever.

This is important, for we have a responsibility when we seek to give socialism prestige, to show what socialism can do, to improve socialism, to make socialism more efficient. We have achieved a lot, we have performed great feats, but there is still much to be done, we have a long way to go, we still have a lot of successes to achieve.

If you see someone trying to enter our country illegally to spy or to commit acts of sabotage or a crime, you fight him resolutely. If you see a landing craft arriving on our coasts, you immediately go out to fight them because they are attacking our physical security. If you see enemy planes starting to bomb us, you won't hesitate a moment to open fire because you see that they are invading us, that they are attacking us. That's how we must fight against everything that weakens us, against everything that tarnishes socialism's prestige, against everything that makes it less efficient.

Socialism is a new system, it is only a few decades old. Errors have been made under socialism; yes, lots of errors of all kinds throughout its history. This is understandable and also inevitable, and we must learn all the lessons of these errors so we can avoid them. The people of Cuba could say with satisfaction that they have not committed many of the errors committed by others. [*Applause*] We have made errors and we have to rectify starting from our own errors. We should not rectify starting from the errors made by others but from our own errors, from our own experiences. [*Applause*]

And we have the duty to fight against anything that weakens the revolution, just as we would fight an enemy landing on our soil, because we have to demonstrate the superiority of socialism in every field. We have seen that superiority many times, not only in our excellent schools or in some medical centers, not only in the great social achievements, but also in the field of the economy, in the field of production. We see what people are capable of and what we are capable of achieving.

Recently I visited a number of places throughout the country. I visited the machine plant in Camagüey, where there are almost 4,000 workers, young people whose average age is twenty-four; over 450 of them are university graduates. It is an extraordinary workplace created by the revolution, proof of what the revolution can do, and it constitutes a real hope.

We've seen it in the contingents that are building roads and working thirteen and fourteen hours a day. They are doing what no group of workers does or can do under capitalism: rationally using resources and machines, obtaining extraordinary results. We've seen it in Granma Province, in groups of workers that have received their banners and are building dams for rice plantations, for sugarcane, to produce food for the population. We granted banners to three brigades! Among them were many internationalist compañeros.

We saw it in Las Tunas Province, at a rolling mill that was built in seventeen months from the time the decision was made, built in Cuba and which will produce steel rods for construction. It has a young work force and was built by a contingent that completed it in fourteen months and says that the next one will be finished in twelve months. We see that really extraordinary things can be done, things that can never be done under capitalism. [*Applause*]

We are taking advantage of all these possibilities, of all this strength. Let us wage a generalized battle against mediocrity, irresponsibility, indolence, and negligence.

Whatever is wrong here is our own fault, yours and ours, each worker's at his job and each leader's. And if what is wrong is our own fault we have to scrutinize ourselves closely, we have to struggle consistently against our own deficiencies, our own negligence, our own indolence.

Even though this has always been our duty, it is our duty today more than ever, because today our country has great international responsibilities, great responsibilities! Not because it is a great power, but because it is a great example of revolutionary spirit, of internationalism, of heroism, of bravery in its ability to confront the empire, in its audacity to build socialism right next door to the empire.

Our country has a great responsibility in Latin America, in this crucial hour for Latin America. Cuba is listened to more and more. Cuba's prestige increases by the day, not only in Latin America but in the world. And at this difficult time for socialism, when the empire is using all its ideological means to try to raise questions and to create confusion, we have the sacred patriotic mission and the sacred internationalist mission of raising as high as possible the banners of socialism, the potential of socialism, the prestige of socialism. [*Applause*]

Working better and more efficiently is good not only for our country but for the world. It is good for our cause, it is good for our ideology, and, above all, it is good for the peoples of Latin America and the Third World. It is good for all peoples, even the peoples of the socialist countries, and it is also good for the workers of the capitalist countries.

Let us hold our heads higher than ever! Let us raise these banners higher than ever! Let us give them more prestige than ever! For if the empire takes pleasure in thinking that socialism's prestige is declining, or that the socialist system will fail, more than ever must we show the empire what socialism is capable of. Now more than ever must we show it, in times of difficulty. [*Applause*]

Defending banners in easy times is not difficult at all, it's nothing particularly worthy of merit. Defending banners in difficult times—that is what's really worthy of merit. Defending socialism when it's in fashion or at the peak of its prestige is easy. Defending socialism when it's having difficulties on the international scene—that is a task worthy of merit. Defending socialism when there are not only international difficulties but national difficulties as well—that is what is most worthy of merit. And we have to defend socialism now that there are international difficulties as well as national difficulties. Some of these difficulties are derived from our own errors; others are derived from situations beyond our control.

Our errors lie in not having done more over the same time period, in not having done things better during these thirty years, in having made mistakes, some of which stemmed from imitating the experience of other socialist countries, from imitating the experience of other countries, many of whom are now saying that their experience was no good. We don't want them telling us in ten or twenty years that some of the things they're doing today are no good.

That's why we must start from our own experiences, our

own ideas, our own interpretations of Marxism-Leninism. Interpreting Marxism-Leninism in a creative and original manner, not letting ourselves be weighed down by dogmas is what led us to victory, is what led us to where we are now.

But the difficulties derived from our own errors must not lead us to discouragement, just as the difficulties derived from the errors that are not ours should not discourage us. We should not be discouraged by the objective conditions existing in the world of today, where billions of people are plundered by the neocolonial and imperialist powers. We should not be discouraged by problems that are objective, that affect humanity as a whole, that affect the countries of Latin America and the Third World in particular. On the contrary, we should raise our voices to summon all our peoples to a common struggle to overcome these objective difficulties.

We should be prepared to overcome any obstacle. If the road were smooth, if it were easy, then there would be no honor, no glory in being called a revolutionary; there would be no dignity, no pride in being considered a revolutionary.

We must be prepared to face all difficulties and all acts of aggression and to struggle on all fronts. As I said, we must do so not only in the military field but in the political and ideological fields as well.

Under these circumstances, strengthening confidence in the [Communist] party and the unity behind the party is more important than ever. [*Applause*] I say unity behind the party, behind our party and our party's point of view. Parties can make mistakes, they can have weaknesses; what we have to do is correct them, overcome the mistakes. But whoever tries to destroy our faith in the party is undermining the foundations of our confidence, the foundations of our strength.

Whoever weakens the party's authority will be weakening the revolution's authority. Without a party there can be no revolution, without a party there can be no socialism.

[*Applause and shouts*] Without the party and without its authority, the process would not be able to make any progress. That's why it is our revolution's duty to give the party more and more authority. It is the members' duty to more and more watch over the party's prestige and authority.

Discipline today is more indispensable than ever. Anyone who promotes or commits social indiscipline is supporting the enemy, is a conscious or unconscious agent of the enemy.

That's why all those manifestations of indiscipline, all those wrongdoings, everything done badly, everything immoral or illegal must be forcefully combated everywhere, [*Applause*] because these things are like the crews on board the landing craft nearing our coasts to invade the country; they are the fifth column, the agents, the servants of the empire's ideology, of capitalism's ideology, of the counter-revolution's ideology.

I repeat: What is done badly, wrongdoing, sloppiness, negligence, social indiscipline, and I would also say delinquency are, in the ideological sphere, like landing craft nearing our coasts to invade our country. In other words, we must wage a battle in the ideological field, a battle in the political field, a daily battle in the construction of socialism, a daily battle for efficiency, because the other battle is more easily seen.

If planes come here to bomb us, if ships come to fire cannons at us, if soldiers come to land here, the military battle is easier to see than the other battle. The enemy is easier to identify on a battlefield than in the field of economics, in the field of politics, in the field of ideology.

That's why today we must reflect on this, on the need to defend ourselves in every field, on the need to be armed in every field, ready for defense in every sphere, and without letting any difficulty discourage us.

We are fighting against objective and material difficulties and we are trying to overcome them. The battle is not easy. The difficulties may even increase. We're going through a very special situation.

New experiments, new experiences, all kinds of reforms are taking place in the socialist camp, especially in the USSR. If they are successful, it will be good for socialism and for everyone else. If they have serious difficulties, the consequences will be especially hard for us. Thus, we may be in for difficulties from the enemy camp and difficulties from the camp of our own friends. But not even this will be able to discourage us.

Precisely today, thirty-two years ago, on December 5, we had our worst setback in the whole war.[17] At about this time I was with two other men, Raúl [Castro] was with another handful of compañeros, there was hardly anything left of our army, nothing worse could have been conceived. Yet none of us was discouraged. We were determined to go on fighting and we did. We were determined to reach victory and we did. We were determined to continue the struggle and we did. And that's why now millions of men and women like you have been able to organize and arm yourselves. [Applause]

That's why today we have a party made up of hundreds of thousands of members, plus the hundreds of thousands of members of the Union of Young Communists, plus the millions of men and women who work in our countryside, in our factories, and in our service industries. What I want to say is that we are men of struggle, that we are men who have never been discouraged by any difficulty because we have known how to live through the most difficult times. And if we were able to win when we were only a handful that could be counted on one's fingers, now that we are millions, there can be no kind of force, external or internal, there can be no objective or subjective difficulties capable of stopping our victorious and definitive march toward the future!

Patria o muerte! [Homeland or death!]

Venceremos! [We will win!]

[*Ovation*]

The Cuban people will always remain loyal to the principles of socialism

January 1, 1989

Fellow citizens of Santiago and all of Cuba:

I believe this was more or less how I addressed you the first time, when the revolution triumphed.

It had been decided to officially commemorate the thirtieth anniversary in the city of Havana. It had been some time since an event of this nature had been held in the capital. In addition, we did not want to confront the difficulties of having the commemoration in the city of Santiago de Cuba, where a big effort would have been necessary for transporting and accommodating the many guests taking part in the commemoration. However, as a really very special wish I proposed to the comrades organizing the anniversary program the idea of visiting Santiago today at this time. It

This speech was given to a rally in Santiago de Cuba, Cuba's second largest city, in the southeastern part of the island. It was held at the same spot where Castro spoke exactly thirty years before to a mass rally after Batista had fled Cuba and the Rebel Army had entered the city.

seemed to me we wouldn't be properly commemorating the thirtieth anniversary if we couldn't at least spend some time here with you, the people of Santiago de Cuba, to convey to you our fraternal greetings. [*Applause*]

I did not come here to recount the great effort carried out by the people of Santiago de Cuba Province over the past thirty years; that was already done a few months ago, on July 26. Neither am I here to recount the work of the revolution over thirty years—I recall that was done at the twenty-fifth anniversary and at the time Santiago de Cuba was awarded the status of Heroic City.

I came here to share with you this glorious day and to recall with you that day thirty years ago where, from this very balcony, in this very square, we celebrated victory. [*Applause*] That ceremony was perhaps not as solemn, not as well-organized as this one—you understand how those days were—but it was truly moving and historic. I believe that many people remember it, and that in addition many have heard about it at times from their parents or teachers. That was a really historic day and I think it will also be an unforgettable day, not just for us—that goes without saying—but also for future generations.

January 1 marked not just the culmination of a long effort of struggle by our people over the course of many years, over nearly 100 years at that time. That day was not just the day of victory; it was also a day of great decisions, fundamental decisions, and a day of great definitions, great lessons, and great training. Because on January 1 victory was not only won, it also had to be defended.

At dawn on that day in 1959, while we were in the town of Contramaestre—or rather at the sugar mill located there—we heard what we could say were the first rumors that the dictatorship had collapsed or rather that Batista had fled the country. A few minutes later the news began to be confirmed. We immediately realized what was going on because prior to this a series of important events had taken place.

The war had already been won. Three days earlier a meeting was held that had been requested previously—around December 25—by the head of the enemy troops in the country's eastern region, General Eulogio Cantillo. This officer was not known for being repressive or for being involved in bloody events. For the benefit of historical truth, it must be said that during the time he was in charge of operations and, above all, during the last offensive launched against the Sierra Maestra, this officer was not known for bloody repression. He was rather considered to be a relatively decent officer.

We had already exchanged some communications with him earlier, mainly concerning the release of enemy prisoners in the hands of our troops, both before and after the offensive.[1] Before the offensive he had even sent us an apparently gentlemanly message voicing his concern and regret for the operation he was about to launch with 10,000 soldiers supported by artillery, armored vehicles and, above all, aircraft, against our strongholds in the Sierra Maestra, and which he viewed as unstoppable and irresistible. He went so far as to voice his regret that persons whom he considered valuable would be lost.

We thanked him very modestly, and very modestly told him we were waiting for his army in the Sierra Maestra. We also told him, of course, that if they succeeded in overcoming the tenacious resistance they were going to encounter and if they succeeded in exterminating the Rebels to the last man, that it shouldn't cause him pain, for the day would come when even the children of the very soldiers fighting us would look to the Sierra Maestra with admiration. I didn't want to tell him what we were certain would happen, that the offensive would be defeated in spite of the extremely limited number of men we had at the time, not even 300. That's why I said that we thanked him modestly and conveyed that answer to him.

Later other contacts took place, especially at the end of the offensive, which became a military disaster for the dictatorship. During the return of enemy prisoners new contacts took place. So this was the background.

On many occasions throughout the war we sent messages to Batista's troops and to some of their leaders. Around December 25 Cantillo requested to meet with us and the meeting took place on December 28. We were already preparing the advance on Santiago de Cuba and he told us they had lost the war—they openly admitted it—and that they were prepared to bring the fighting to an end.

We told him that the issue now was to find a practical way to put a stop to the war. In reality we were generous because we said that the army was sunk and that perhaps a number of officers not involved with crimes could be saved. So I proposed to him that in order to bring the fighting to an end in an honorable manner, an uprising should take place among the troops in Oriente Province—the former Oriente Province—mainly the troops of the Santiago de Cuba garrison, and that it should appear to be a revolutionary military movement that brought the fighting to an end, adding that such an event would immediately topple the dictatorship.

We warned him—as we had always warned throughout the fighting—that we were resolutely against any kind of coup d'état. We preached this constantly throughout the war, based on the experience of Latin America and of Cuba itself. Because in the past, great struggles had been waged against tyrannical governments and at a given moment a group of army officers always turned up, toppling the government and presenting themselves as saviors of the nation.

Bearing that experience in mind, all throughout the war we maintained a policy of rejecting, condemning, and discouraging any military coup; we had warned that if a military coup took place we would continue the war. We made these statements at various times—when we had 100 men, when we had 150, when we had 200, and we reiterated it up to the end of the war.

So agreement was reached for the Santiago de Cuba uprising to begin at 3:00 p.m. on December 31. But Cantillo kept insisting he had to travel to Havana and we were opposed to that. He claimed he had an important number of contacts, even arguing that he had a close relative in an important military position at the head of one of the western regiments. We advised him not to make the trip; he insisted on the need for it, the importance of it, whereupon we issued him three warnings: first, that we didn't want a coup d'état in the capital; second, that we didn't want any one to help Batista escape; and third, that we wanted no contact with the American embassy. These were three things we warned him about and that we told him we would not stand for. He solemnly promised not to do any of the three things.

He traveled to the capital—perhaps that same day or the next—and then we began to get strange bits of news, confused messages, stating that we had to wait, at least until January 6. Needless to say, we weren't prepared to accept changes in what we had agreed upon, given that our troops were advancing everywhere, taking over one city after another, blocking the retreat of nearly all the government's troops in the former province of Oriente, and we realized that the right moment had arrived to liberate the city of Santiago de Cuba, to deal, so to speak, the final blow to the regime in the city of Santiago de Cuba. We weren't going to wait six or seven days and let these optimal conditions go to waste. It was always the view and it was always a principle of the Rebel forces to never lose a day, a minute, or a second and, above all, to take advantage of the right psychological moment. And so we sent a message to the deputy chief of the Santiago garrison, telling him we did not accept the unilateral changes of the agreements or the confused explanations given us, and that if there was no uprising of the garrison on the afternoon of December 31, we would begin operations against the city of Santiago de Cuba.

This was our clear warning and, indeed, our forces were advancing on Santiago de Cuba when in the early morning of January 1 we received the news I mentioned earlier.

What did the army want to do at the eleventh hour, unquestionably following the advice of the United States? To carry out a coup d'état, confuse the people, saying: "Batista is gone, the tyranny is over, a democratic era has begun," while keeping the military apparatus intact, maintaining the system, and thus preventing the triumph of the revolution. It was a grotesque attempt at repeating what had happened on other occasions in the history of our country and what had happened so often in many other Latin American countries. So we weren't taken by surprise by what was going on.

It is my understanding that our people, thanks to our constant warnings throughout the war and to the broadcasts over Radio Rebelde, were also alerted to this situation.[2]

They carried out the coup, helped Batista escape, and collaborated with the American embassy. They proclaimed a government to take charge of the situation. It must not be forgotten that on January 1 a government was proclaimed. Those carrying out the coup appointed a Supreme Court justice named Piedra as president of the republic. Actually, that government was not even inaugurated.

That same day we made the decision, without wasting a minute, without wasting a second, to denounce the coup and issue instructions to all Rebel forces to continue operations. We didn't want even a minute of truce between the revolutionary forces and the enemy forces.

And on that January 1 an event occurred that we had foreseen on July 26, 1953. Our plan following the attack on the Moncada garrison was to issue a call to the people for a revolutionary general strike, and the time for calling a revolutionary general strike came precisely on the morning of January 1. I believe that was an exceptional event. All the trade unions were in the hands of official leaders tied to the dictatorship. There was not a single official trade union leadership body working with the revolution.

Immediately after denouncing the coup and issuing the instructions to heads of Rebel columns, a call went out to the people over Radio Rebelde for a general strike. At the same time, a proclamation was broadcast to Santiago de Cuba instructing the city to come to a total stop as of 3:00 p.m., except for the power station, to keep communications open with the population, and we warned the population we would proceed to attack the city. All those decisions were made one after the other on January 1.

At the same time as the Rebels were approaching Santiago de Cuba, Camilo [Cienfuegos] and Che [Guevara] were instructed to advance toward the capital, without stopping and without letup. A group of scouts dispatched along the Central Highway even received orders that as soon as they came to Quintero Hill, where an enemy battalion had been deployed, they should allow five minutes for surrender and then open fire, that there would be no truce.

This was the situation as we approached the city of Santiago de Cuba on the north, from Palma Soriano, when the first contacts took place requested by the heads of the Santiago de Cuba garrison. The police headquarters immediately surrendered; the commanding officers of two heavily armed naval frigates docked in the Santiago de Cuba port surrendered; the naval district chief surrendered; and the heads of the garrison tried to contact us. All this was happening during the afternoon. Following the first contacts, I told the head of the Santiago de Cuba garrison that I wanted to meet with all the officers in the garrison.

Those were very important steps because we didn't know what was going to happen in the capital; whether they had succeeded in keeping the support of a large part of the army, whether fighting would break out in the capital of the republic owing to a substantial number of officers and troops supporting the coup.

Liberating the city of Santiago de Cuba was of enormous importance, and seizing the weapons they had here in Santiago de Cuba would be decisive, as we saw it. Above all, we wanted to avoid bloodshed, because the fighting, no doubt, would have been violent.

We figured that the fighting around Santiago de Cuba—that was before the coup—would last about a week. We had already organized an uprising of the city during the final stage of the battle—more than 100 weapons had been brought in from those just captured in Palma Soriano. We had worked out every aspect of how to conduct the Santiago de Cuba operation, which would have ended successfully, no doubt, but at the expense of a number of lives, perhaps a large number of lives.

That's why I think it was decisive, fundamental, and necessary to make every effort to capture the city without combat, if at all possible. If no other alternative was left, then we would capture it in combat, but fortunately circumstances arose that made combat unnecessary in and around Santiago de Cuba.

Anyone might imagine that we revolutionaries wanted to take over the Moncada garrison, to capture it by force of arms, just as we captured many other enemy positions. But under those circumstances no one should let themselves be carried away by emotion; one must try to obtain the goals sought with the least possible cost in human lives. And that was what happened that day.

Analyzing things from a distance one realizes that the enemy army had at the time lost all capacity to resist; it was already totally demoralized. It even turned out that when our scouting patrol came to Quintero Hill no one put up any resistance—it arrived and entered the Moncada garrison.

It so happened that Compañero Raúl [Castro] went there to arrange for the meeting agreed upon with the Santiago de Cuba garrison officers. He entered the garrison, spoke to the officers, tore down a portrait of Batista and ripped it up right in front of all of them, and he also spoke to the troops. [*Applause*] He went with the officers to the meeting they had with me. We didn't mention surrender—because, I repeat again, the situation was very confused at the time—we didn't want to humiliate them. We asked them to condemn the military coup; I denounced the maneuvering of the promoters of the coup; I denounced Cantillo, the man who up to that moment had been their head. I told them about what we had agreed on, his lack of compliance, I called on them to disobey Cantillo's orders and to come over to our side, and they agreed.

I would say it was really a generous proposal on our part and an absolutely correct one, given that developments in the rest of the country still weren't clear.

What interested us were the frigates, the tanks, and the artillery in Santiago de Cuba, and also those who knew how to handle those weapons.

Although its forces had already lost all capacity to resist, the enemy continued its maneuvering. They dispatched a plane to the Isle of Pines—that was its name then—to bring back a group of officers who had plotted against Batista, primarily to bring back a colonel who hadn't really been involved with Batista—he had gained a certain authority precisely for having opposed Batista, for having plotted against him, and he had been kept imprisoned on the Isle of Pines. Since that officer had about him an aura of having fought against the dictatorship, they sent for him in an attempt to hold the army together. The colonel's group was known as the "pure ones"; this was how it was known nationwide.

So they sent for Colonel Barquín, who, in addition, was

very friendly and close to the Yankees, they brought him back to Camp Columbia,[3] and gave him command of the army—all of this, mind you, on January 1. They carried out this move together with the American embassy. And, indeed, the man arrived at Camp Columbia during the night.

As we were assembled here with the people of Santiago de Cuba, the situation had still not been resolved, although by then Camilo and Che were advancing on the capital during the night. It has not yet been pinpointed at what exact minute they set out on their advance. But I do remember—although I can't pinpoint the exact hour—when this colonel, the new chief of the army who replaced Cantillo, wanted to reach me on the telephone. (Cantillo stepped down after surrendering command to this officer.) But my reply was that I would speak with no one in Camp Columbia except Camilo, once he was in command of the camp. [*Applause*]

All these events were happening that night, and then, as soon as the rally here in this plaza had concluded, we took the tanks and the artillery and, gaining strength, we advanced on Bayamo. We had to see what was happening with the Bayamo troops; the situation wasn't entirely clear, and no one knew what might happen. Upon reaching Bayamo I met with the troops there; I spoke to them and they joined us. They had bigger tanks with heavier guns, they had artillery. All this was happening around the morning of January 3. I was then heading toward Havana leading a column of 1,000 Rebels and 2,000 Batista soldiers, artillery, and tanks.

Although journalists and historians have so far conducted some extensive research and done a very good job in recording the historical events of those days, I think that still more things and more details ought to be pinpointed more exactly—the hour Camilo left for the capital, the hour Che left, the exact day and hour of their arrival at Camp Columbia and the La Cabaña fortress respectively, and at what time they got the situation under control there.

On January 2, as our forces were approaching the capital as quickly as possible in view of what could happen there, the troops of Camilo and Che were advancing along the highway and capturing garrisons without combat. So the effort to get a leading figure out of jail, capable of holding the army together and boosting its morale, was to no avail.

I don't remember the exact date, but already by January 3 things were becoming clear and it was evident there would be no more resistance. Of course, heeding the call of the Rebel Army broadcast over Radio Rebelde, the general strike paralyzed the country from one end to the other in an impressive manner.

That strike played an extremely important role; it was a tremendous blow. It completely demoralized the enemy forces, avoided bloodshed, and saved lives. The workers of the radio and television networks hooked up with Radio Rebelde and at a certain point Radio Rebelde was broadcasting to the entire country by radio and television over all the stations. The people were mobilized everywhere and in the capital itself.

All these events turned out to be important because they helped to quash the enemy maneuver and ushered in the victory of the revolution, a total and complete victory.

One can say that in seventy-two hours all the country's garrisons were under control and the weapons were in the hands of the people. In the span of a few days tens of thousands of compañeros had armed themselves. One can say that the army was disarmed, although not entirely, because certain units kept their weapons—above all, the units that had agreed to support us, that had committed themselves to us, and that for a time kept their weapons. At a later stage of the revolution it became impossible to keep them armed, as the imperialist conspiracies and counterrevolutionary plots began in our country.

Camilo and Che carried out their missions and at a certain

moment they had control over the capital's military forces. Then our journey toward the capital became more a political tour than a military one.

All these things, or the great majority of them that I mentioned, occurred on January 1. Not only was it the day of victory, it was also the day of the counterattack, the coup d'état, the general strike, the advance to defend the victory, and it was a day of fundamental decisions and important definitions.

I recall all these things with the aim of pointing out the extremely important role played by the city of Santiago de Cuba that day. [*Applause*] The fact that the enemy knew that it was faced by a militant, rebellious, and heroic population was a very important factor in helping to break down the morale of Batista's forces occupying Santiago de Cuba.

They had about 5,000 men, while the forces with which we were getting ready to capture the city numbered 1,200. Nobody thought that was too few; it was the time when we had the largest number of forces available to us, it was the best ratio of our forces to theirs we ever had: slightly more than one to every five enemy soldiers. Of course, we never pitted one soldier against five; we always employed the tactic of striking at specific points, creating favorable situations for our forces.

But we had two armies: the Rebel Army and the army of the people, [*Applause*] the men, women, workers, students, and young people of Santiago de Cuba, and the enemy could not withstand the pressure.

That event and what happened in Santiago de Cuba on the afternoon of January 1—the people pouring into the streets, the impressive rally that night, our denunciation of what had happened, of the disloyalty of that military commander and the maneuver—played a key role in those events and must have exerted a considerable influence on the total demoralization of the enemy forces in the capital as well, which was

900 kilometers away. But our army, which was speedy and energetic, had also advanced those 900 kilometers.

I have often tried to calculate—it isn't easy to do so precisely—how many men under arms we had on that January 1. It was about 3,000; Batista's army, including the navy and the police, numbered about 80,000 at the time. Therefore I want to stress the role that day not only of the fighters but also of the people and the workers. [*Applause*]

It's not that the city was passively liberated and was given over solely to applause or expressions of jubilation. The city had struggled for many years to make possible that day of liberation. Our people throughout the country—and, of course, in the capital—played an important role over the years, an active and heroic one. However, due to a series of circumstances Santiago became a protagonist of great importance in the struggle.

Other cities such as Bayamo, Manzanillo, and Guantánamo also played important roles throughout our war of liberation. [*Applause*] But our struggle had begun in Santiago on July 26, 1953, and from that time on Santiago had expressed solidarity with the revolution.

Santiago had exerted influence over us even before July 26, because at the time of Batista's coup on March 10, 1952, the only city in Cuba where there were important popular movements and where the coup took the longest to consolidate control was Santiago de Cuba. [*Applause*]

We could say that Santiago had influenced us throughout our lives as did the eastern provinces as a whole, because of their important role in the history of our homeland. That history started even before a nation existed, when foreign invaders occupied the island. It was in these eastern provinces where the Indians, extraordinarily peaceful and kind by nature, offered the first example of courage and heroism against the foreign invasion. The first cities were founded here and even when the first settlements existed, when the feelings of nationality had just begun to be formed, the struggles for independence began in these provinces. The first and second wars of independence—the third, if you wish to count the Little War—all these took place in the eastern provinces. The cities of these provinces played a singular role in our wars for liberation, especially Santiago de Cuba. [*Applause*]

In the eastern region, formerly Oriente Province, there occurred one of the most admirable, amazing, and instructive incidents in our history, the Baraguá Protest. [*Applause*] It was undertaken by a son of the city of Santiago de Cuba, Antonio Maceo. [*Prolonged applause*] From this city came that group of lions, the sons of Mariana Grajales, as well as many other distinguished fighters and patriots.[4]

These eastern traditions played a key role in the history of our country. I believe that one correct evaluation of our generation and our revolutionary group was our conviction that this tradition of struggle, dignity, rebelliousness, love of freedom and independence remained alive in this part of the country. Of course, we felt those sentiments existed throughout the country, but they were strongest in the eastern region. It was a correct evaluation because it helped us to drive forward our struggle, to select the terrain and the geography of our struggle, the ideal topographical and human location for our struggles, all of which were closely intertwined.

These aren't just things to come and say in Santiago de Cuba on January 1. They were demonstrated by facts more than thirty years ago. When we organized the attack on the Moncada garrison with young men from the western provinces—magnificent, dedicated, heroic, and disciplined men—we recruited only one from Santiago. This, of course, was to confuse the enemy so they would have no idea as to where we planned to strike. But we picked Santiago de Cuba and its garrison for one simple reason. Why didn't we recruit Santiago residents? Because we already counted on them beforehand. [*Prolonged applause*] We knew we would have the support of Santiago de Cuba. Otherwise why attack the Moncada garrison and try to capture thousands of weapons? Who were those weapons going to be for? For the residents of Santiago de Cuba.

Such was our confidence in the heroic traditions, courage, and rebelliousness of the city that influenced us long before the Moncada, because it was the part of the country that we knew best, it was where we had grown up, the part of the country linked to our best feelings and affection. But Santiago de Cuba and the eastern region were important long before we were born; they had an influence on the life and history of the country.

I have always felt that one of the most beautiful and glorious pages of history is the one written by our people for over 100 years. And I believe that if there was one heroic war, much more heroic than any other, it was our Ten Years War. [*Applause*] The last of our wars of independence in the nineteenth century was just as extraordinary. And I believe that we must make known this rich and marvelous wellspring of history to children, adolescents, students, young people, the people as a whole. It must never be forgotten because it was from that history that today's Cuba was born.

I have often explained to foreign visitors how Cuba was the last to free itself from Spain, how when Bolívar, San Martín, O'Higgins, Sucre, Hidalgo, Morelos, and so many other patriots wrote the history of the independence of the Americas—a huge world that fought together against colonialism during the difficult period of Spanish history in the wake of Napoleon's invasion, when a French king had even been imposed on Spain—at that special conjuncture the independence movement of Latin America got under way and all those countries struggling more or less simultaneously achieved independence.

At that time Cuba was a slave-owning society, a slave-owning society! There were hundreds of thousands of slaves, chiefly in the western region of the country. The Spanish controlled trade and administration plus they had absolute control of the armed forces and police. The so-called creoles owned the sugar and coffee plantations and didn't even want to hear of independence. They were terrified by the idea of independence, above all after the slave uprising in Haiti—which by the way was the first country in Latin America to become free, before Bolívar, long before Bolívar; it rose up against the mighty French empire, against no less than the troops of Napoleon Bonaparte. The creoles were terrified that something similar could happen here and they thought that all talk of independence jeopardized their status as a privileged social class.

That was the origin of annexationism. It was then that a whole social sector began to look to the north. At the same time annexationist feelings also developed in the United States. The southern states were in conflict with the industrialized states of the northeast; the southern states opposed an end to slavery and wanted another slave state in the United States.

In the past, when they always fooled us in every way possible, they told us that Narciso López had been a forerunner of the independence struggle.[5] Historical truth shows he came to Cuba with the encouragement, sponsorship, and supplies provided by the southern slave states of the United States and there was no thought of independence; on the contrary the idea was annexation. Destiny contributed to the cause of independence, because those expeditions were defeated. The flag we salute with such well-deserved respect was first unfurled by the annexationists. Today it is our sovereign flag because our immortal independence fighters made it sovereign and heroic in the independence wars that began in 1868. [*Applause*]

Look at the lessons of history, the things that can happen when there is confusion. However, our people were able to overcome all that confusion. The annexationist movement lasted for a long while and in a certain sense annexationist sentiment existed throughout the entire history of the republic. What are all those capitalists, landlords, rich sectors, and confused sectors or confused people if not holdovers of the slave-owning era, when the rich did not even want a homeland?

However, there emerged in our history outstanding men who, although wealthy, wanted a homeland and were willing to sacrifice their wealth for the country, such as Carlos Manuel de Céspedes, Vicente Aguilera, Ignacio Agramonte, and many others. [*Applause*] They started their liberation struggles here in these provinces, where there were fewer slaves. The bulk of the slaves were in the western region of the country, where the biggest sugar and coffee plantations were in the first half of the nineteenth century.

The struggle for independence started here, where there were more free peasants and fewer slave owners, where the rich were less reactionary, where some plantation owners had developed national feelings, a national identity, an idea of nationhood. Nevertheless, when the war of independence began there was still some confusion in Cuban political thinking, as shown in the early months of the 1868 war—I discussed this during the centennial celebration of the Cry of Yara. But just look at the importance of these ideas and concepts, of the importance of clear ideas at each decisive stage in our history; because holdovers of those times still remain, although much less. In particular we again witness the identification between the interests of the exploiting classes and proimperialist and antipatriotic views. Thus the importance of history and ideas.

I think that on a day such as this it's worth recalling that the noble and patriotic ideas that took root in the people of the eastern region played a key role, a decisive role, in the last war of liberation.

I forgot to mention among the historic events that started in this province the immortal feat of the westward invasion by the forces of Maceo and Máximo Gómez.[6] [*Applause*]

All these events and factors had a tremendous influence on our history and on our last struggle for liberation. I think that all those ideas and feelings were merged on January 1, 1959.

It must be said that this spirit has continued over the last thirty years. What made possible the historic feat of the internationalist missions by our revolutionary people? What made possible the conduct of our forces in Cuito Cuanavale, [*Prolonged applause*] the resolute advance of our forces in southwestern Angola, the victories at Techipa, Calueque, and others that led to the recently signed peace agreements? What made possible this marvelous spirit of internationalism, this unselfishness, this exemplary solidarity by the Cuban people in the face of every difficult task and every challenge? It was those feelings that began to take root in Yara, those patriotic and internationalist feelings; the feelings that began to take root in Baraguá and continued in Baire,[7] that continued at the Moncada and the *Granma,* and that emerged victorious on January 1, 1959. [*Applause*]

The history of a country is not written in a day and national feelings are not forged overnight. Our feelings and history were not forged overnight. But I am convinced that these feelings have reached a very high plane, a very high plane! [*Applause*] We can now be proud of them and I'm sure our forefathers would also be proud, those who fought in the wars of independence, those *mambís* who planted the fertile seed,[8] those who fought and died throughout our history, those who fought and died at the Moncada, in the *Granma,* and in the Sierra Maestra, as well as those who shed their generous blood in the noble and unequaled internationalist missions undertaken by our people. [*Applause*]

The heroic and glorious Baraguá Protest was not in vain because it taught us revolutionary intransigence and loyalty to principles; the blood shed by Martí was not in vain because it also taught us revolutionary intransigence and loyalty to principles. [*Applause*] I am sure they dreamed of a people such as this. [*Applause*]

That's the meaning of a January 1 whose moral and historical dimensions cannot be fully grasped no matter how often they are mentioned or repeated. In the light of all this we are even more proud of the banner and the title of Heroic City granted to this city and with it, to the eastern provinces of the country. [*Prolonged applause*]

Today we recall the thirtieth anniversary perhaps in a calmer manner than on that day, but more aware than ever of our strength, more convinced than ever of the infinite moral qualities of our people, more convinced than ever that these provinces will be invincible bastions of the revolution, [*Applause*] as is all of Cuba now, where the seed of your example has taken root. [*Applause*] Our people are more united than ever with these historic ties. It was no accident that the city of Havana sent us Martí, who died at Dos Ríos, whose remains rest with such love in this city, and it is no accident that Santiago sent Antonio Maceo to Havana, [*Applause*] whose remains today are like a temple for our citizens in the west.

Therefore, compañeras and compañeros of Santiago, veterans of our struggles, men and women, adolescents, young and old, students, workers, eastern fighters, we are very, very pleased to inaugurate the fourth decade of the victorious revolution here in Santiago de Cuba. [*Prolonged applause*]

Those who dream that the revolution may perhaps be swept away are fooling themselves. Those who dream such folly fail to realize that the revolution, which is the continuation of our country's history, its highest stage, one might say, will celebrate its fortieth, fiftieth, sixtieth, and one hundredth anniversaries, and many more. Of this we have no doubt. [*Applause*]

More than once we will have to refurbish this building; perhaps we will have to strengthen these balconies. But I am sure that on each of those anniversaries somebody will come to talk about January 1, 1959. [*Applause and shouts of "Fidel, Fidel, Fidel!"*]

What were we on that January 1, apart from the courage and valor of our people and combatants; apart from the desire for freedom and the will to build a new homeland?

How many engineers, draftsmen, agronomists, veterinarians, teachers, professors, doctors, specialists, officers, cadres, members of the Communist Party and the Union of Young Communists, how many trade unions and mass organizations did we have? We didn't have any of that when we were writing one of the most glorious pages in our history over these thirty years. These were years that started as a struggle against the privileged in our country, against the puppets, against the mercenary army, against landlords and exploiters of all kinds, and ended up being a struggle against aggression, threats, blockades, and the power of the strongest empire in the history of humanity.

We are here because we've known how to resist over these thirty years, something few perhaps believed could happen, something perhaps nobody could ever have imagined. Here we are after thirty years of difficult, courageous, and intelligent struggle by our people in the face of all threats and risks. That was our greatest accomplishment and we couldn't even dream of having what we have now: hundreds of thousands of teachers, professors, and technicians; tens of thousands of engineers, draftsmen, agronomists, specialists of all kinds; tens of thousands of doctors who now protect the health of our people, ten times more than the number we were left with when the revolution triumphed. We have a tremendous intellectual and technical force; a sound, vigorous, and magnificent youth responsible for the feats of this decade—youth who I am sure are better and more capable of firmness and heroism. [*Applause*]

With this and with the extraordinary experience accumulated by our people over these thirty years we can face the future, and if a lot has been done—errors and shortcomings notwithstanding—we can do even more in the future, because I'm sure that with what we have we can transform every year into two, three, and four years, and that's what we are now trying to do.

That January 1 was a day of definitions, in which we said something that still had to be said. In view of the long record of deceit and corrupt politicians throughout the period of the pseudorepublic we had to say that this time we were serious, that a coup d'état could not be confused with a revolution. That was one of the big things our people learned on that January 1, when they confronted and defeated the maneuver. Because our people wanted change, our people wanted a revolution, and the changes had to be deep-going and fundamental, the exploiting society had to disappear. And we told the people that this time the revolution had triumphed, that the demands of the revolution would be fulfilled!

I will never forget that this was the essence of what we said on January 1, how in the wake of the attack on the Moncada garrison the basic objectives and principles of our revolution were proclaimed. That happened twice in Santiago de Cuba: in the hospital where we were tried for the events at the Moncada garrison, and here on January 1. Today with deep conviction I will state that our revolution, our genuine revolution, will continue to advance. And it is a genuine revolution because it is a socialist revolution and because it is a Marxist-Leninist revolution. [*Applause*]

Socialism was something that could not yet be mentioned on that January 1, because of the McCarthyism prevailing in this hemisphere and the rabid anticommunism in the mass media and all the bourgeois institutions, amidst the prevailing confusion. But the revolution didn't delay much in talking about socialism, because we said that this is a genuine revolution and there can be no genuine revolution in our country if it isn't socialist.

So on that April 16, two and a half years after January 1, when our combatants were preparing to confront the mercenary invasion and perhaps imperialist aggression, we proclaimed the socialist character of our revolution. [*Applause*] And not much later we were not only talking about socialism, but we proclaimed the Marxist-Leninist character of our socialist revolution. [*Applause*]

Today, thirty years after that January 1, 1959, we can safely say that our people will always remain loyal to the principles of socialism! [*Applause*] That our people will always remain loyal to the principles of Marxism-Leninism! [*Applause*] That our people will always remain loyal to the principles of internationalism! [*Applause*] And that staunchly loyal to these principles we will struggle and work to make our revolution better and better, and more and more efficient. [*Applause*]

In these times of confusion, our revolution—which so scares reactionaries everywhere and which so scares the empire—is like a beacon of light in the eyes of the world. At such a time and on this January 1, we can state that we're aware of the tremendous responsibility our revolutionary process has toward the peoples of the world, toward the workers of the world, and especially toward the peoples of the Third World. And we can state that we will always act in keeping with that responsibility. [*Applause*]

Today, therefore, with more vigor than ever, we say: So-

cialism or death! Marxism-Leninism or death! [*Applause*]
That is what is now meant by what we've repeated so often
over these years:

Patria o muerte!
Venceremos! [*Ovation*]

DAVID DEUTSCHMANN

MARY-ALICE WATERS

January 4, 1989, rally in Havana marking the thirtieth anniversary of the Cuban Revolution. Above, Castro awards certificate for exemplary voluntary work; below, members of the Blas Roca construction contingent in the crowd.

Thirty years of
the Cuban revolution

January 4, 1989

Distinguished guests;
Fellow citizens:

I don't know how the acoustics are here. It's not such a
big gathering, but there are many people seated and the
place extends way back. I don't know whether those over
there at the back can hear well. I think they said they can,
right? [*Laughter*]

It will take a bit of patience on the part of those attending
this ceremony who are behind the press, which constitutes a
sort of wall over there. There must be a few dozen or hundreds who can't see the rostrum, but I hope they'll remain
there quietly and not talk too much among themselves.

In the first place, I wish to thank the hundreds and hun-

*This speech was given at the main rally commemorating the thirtieth
anniversary of the revolution, held in Havana's Plaza of the Revolution
before a crowd of more than a hundred thousand. The event also inaugurated ExpoCuba, Havana's new exhibition center, and the Botanical
Gardens.*

dreds of foreign visitors—although perhaps foreign visitors is not the right term and it would be better to call them brothers and sisters from other countries [*Applause*]—who have come to our country to join us in commemorating this historic date and this happy birthday, the thirtieth anniversary of the revolution.

When I say "happy" I don't mean that everything is done and all is well. It means we're happy to arrive at the thirtieth anniversary of the revolution, and we're infinitely grateful for your presence here, given that the revolution was not just the result of our work but also, to a large extent, the result of international support and cooperation. For if this pygmy that is the island of Cuba was able to successfully face up to the imperialist giant, it has to be said that it would not have been possible without the support of the socialist countries and the progressive and democratic forces of the entire world.

I'm not going to make a long and tedious recounting here of the revolution's deeds, works, and successes. I would do better to ask you to forgive us if at a rally like this those of us speaking here praise our own work too much. But that's what happens at every birthday: no child or teenager on their birthday is criticized for any defect; instead their virtues are emphasized. Perhaps a few things ought to be mentioned here in general terms for our foreign guests concerning the colossal efforts made by our country and some of the results achieved.

I'll begin by mentioning what our enemies mention first, namely, education and public health, because our enemies say that we have had colossal successes in education and in health—although some super-renegades have even dared to question whether or not we've had successes in education, health, and sports. Perhaps later on I'll explain why they speak about these things, and it's precisely to deny other things. They can't deny what is so visible.

Our country doesn't have many statistics available concerning the past. It hasn't been easy to find data, since it was nonexistent. A census was made in 1953—the year in which, to be exact, our struggle began; at that time the military dictatorship of Fulgencio Batista had been ruling the country for almost a year. So some of the statistics come from that census.

For instance, it was said that 24 percent of the country's population was illiterate, according to the standards of illiteracy prevailing at the time, because an illiterate was considered to be anyone who didn't know how to sign his name, or add, or write anything, not even a paragraph. Nowadays, according to modern standards, many people who didn't fit that definition of illiteracy are considered illiterates. That is, under more benign estimates and in accordance with narrower standards of illiteracy, there were then close to 24 percent.

I believe that in accordance with modern standards of calculating illiteracy, we could say that our country then had a 60 or 70 percent illiteracy rate.

The average educational level was second grade. Nowhere in the world today is a person with a second-grade education considered anything but an illiterate. That is, of those considered literate many finished only second or third grade and hardly knew how to sign their names.

Primary school attendance, according to that 1953 census, was between 45 and 46 percent, I think, and secondary school attendance came to only around 8 percent. Technological education was practically nonexistent. There were six or seven trade schools, as they were then called.

There were between 10,000 and 15,000 university students, and later, during the period of the Batista dictatorship, practically all the universities were closed down. There was the main university, and another university for the eastern provinces was beginning to be developed, plus some attempts in Camagüey and Holguín. Needless to say, nothing like special schools was known in our country, schools for children with problems and difficulties. And when it came to day-care centers, nothing like that was known in Cuba.

The immense majority of women did not have jobs either, and the jobs they did have were generally very depressing.

In health matters, indices were given. It's estimated—a conservative estimate—that there was a mortality rate of 60 deaths per 1,000 live births in the first year of life. There were no statistics on that; we know it because that was what we had when the statistics began—60 or in the 50s. But no one really knew what the real figure was. We can say that there were more than 60 per 1,000 live births.

The number of mothers who died during delivery exceeded 12 per 10,000.

There were 6,000 doctors in our country. It wasn't a small number, yet they were nearly all concentrated in the capital and many lacked work. We figure that life expectancy was less than sixty. Claiming it was around sixty would be saying too much. There were practically no public health services. A large portion of the population had no access to public health services, and we can say that in the countryside, where over half of the population lived, there were no public health services.

More than 30 percent of the work force was unemployed or underemployed. Social security barely covered 50 percent of the population—and what coverage! In many cases the pensions were insignificant. When the revolution triumphed, there were no retirement funds available; the money had been embezzled.

That was, broadly speaking, the situation that prevailed in our country.

There are some changes that can be mathematically measured, and the international agencies are familiar with the validity of our statistics.

Today, illiteracy has technically—I say technically—been cut to 1.5 percent, that is, it involves people who because of old age or some other problems could not be taught to read and write in any way. Therefore, we can say that illiteracy has been reduced to zero.

Today the opportunity to study extends to 100 percent of the country's children—nationwide—both in the cities and the countryside.

The opportunity to complete a secondary education extends to 100 percent of all the youth who have completed primary education. This doesn't mean that 100 percent of all the children and teenagers avail themselves of this opportunity; it's never 100 percent. There are always some children who for physical or other reasons, including social reasons, don't go to school. That's why we can't say 100 percent; instead it's 99 percent, 98 percent in primary education.

In intermediate-level education—which, as I was saying, covered about 8 percent of young people before the revolution—the opportunity nowadays extends to 100 percent of all young people of those ages. Actually, close to 87 percent go to school in the twelve-to-sixteen age bracket. There are always some cases of teenage marriages, unfortunately. These are things that can't be avoided. Socialism has not yet found the formula for preventing teenage marriages. It tries to promote sexual education, it teaches, educates the young. But there are some factors of a social nature that make it impossible for 100 percent of the young people in the twelve-to-sixteen age bracket to go to school—but never because they don't have the opportunity to go to school.

Nowadays practically every one of the country's fourteen provinces has its own university facilities. In the field of medicine alone, there are twenty-one medical schools in our country. Every province has a medical school—some even have two—and the capital has six. Now every one of the country's fourteen provinces, under the new political-administrative division, trains its own doctors and its own specialists. And there are close to 28,000 students enrolled in the medical schools, which include dentistry and university nursing degrees—I'm talking about education, about university facilities, not about medical services.

There are hundreds of technical schools turning out skilled workers in the country. There are around 100,000 regular university students and more than 200,000 if we consider those who study by alternate means such as workers' guided studies, nurses getting their degrees, primary school teachers getting their primary education degrees, and so on, making a total of 200,000 university students, although many of these are already working. In other words, they will not be future university graduates looking for jobs, but instead they are studying something related to the jobs they already have.

There are more than 1,000 day-care centers in the country, with more than 100,000 children in them, and an ambitious program is under way. Suffice it to say that in 1987, City of Havana Province built 54 day-care centers with an enrollment capacity of 210 children each. And in the year 1988 that just ended, plus a few days into January, the city of Havana finished some 56 more day-care centers: 110 centers in two years. The capital's demand came to 19,500, and there is now capacity for roughly 24,000. Naturally, it's a bit difficult to pinpoint the exact demand because, since there weren't enough available a few years ago, perhaps some people who needed day-care centers did not apply for them.

The country now has available more than 40,000 special education openings, and during the next three or four years an additional 40,000 will be created, which will meet our total special education needs. This is meant for children with hearing or visual problems or learning deficiencies, or there may even be cases of mental retardation and also behavioral problems. In short, for a number of reasons, the need is imposed on society for that kind of special school, which we have already met to a large extent. That is a program begun by the city of Havana.

Havana, with its two million inhabitants, will meet all its special education needs in 1989. And we figure that it may take the rest of the provinces, which are also carrying out their programs, three or four years at the most.

These are truly extraordinary leaps that our country has made in this field. We have a large number of different types of schools ranging from schools for the exact sciences to senior high schools in the countryside, technological schools of various kinds, vocational art schools, and sports schools. Anyway they would be too long to list here, but as I said, I merely wanted to speak about this in broad terms.

In the field of health I can say, for instance, that the infant mortality rate, which in 1987 had been lowered to 13.3 per 1,000 live births in the first year of life, this year, when we hoped to bring it below 13, we managed to take it to less than 12, so that our infant mortality rate for 1988 came to 11.9. This places us—and this rate has been sustained—among the twenty countries with the lowest infant mortality rates in the world, and even below the rates of many industrially developed countries. I think this has truly been an extraordinary accomplishment.

An inland province like Cienfuegos has already dropped to below 10. Last year we were wondering which would be the first province to go below 10—it was Cienfuegos, an inland province, that achieved a rate of 8.9 per 1,000 live births in 1988.

Another inland province, Pinar del Río, known before the revolution as "Cinderella" because of all the calamities they had there, reached a rate of 10. The Isle of Youth reached 10.4, and the capital of the republic had 10.6, which, naturally, makes our capital's infant mortality rate well below that of Washington, the capital of the empire.

Our infant mortality rates are now similar to those of the United States, the world's richest country, which is not among the top countries in low infant mortality rates, of course, although it goes without saying that indeed the affluent, the whites, and so on, may be below 10. But the Black population, the Latinos, Chicanos, all of them, may be as high as 15, 17, 20, or over 20. It's not equal, over there it's not even. When we talk about the infant mortality rate or education in Cuba, we mean all the people in the country, across the board.

There are some provinces that are a bit more advanced, others a bit less, in this question of mortality rates. But they are all progressing in more or less the same way. The highest one is close to 14 but is being lowered—if it isn't 14, it's 15 and is coming down—because I think that it was the province of Las Tunas that last year registered 18 and this year it's around 15. It's advancing. All the provinces are advancing.

The maternal mortality rate in 1988 was 2.6 per 10,000 deliveries—also one of the world's lowest. This gives you an idea of the security that women, mothers, and families have even though the number of deliveries has gone up.

One interesting statistic concerns tuberculosis. The 1988 rate was 5.9 per 100,000 people, which places Cuba below Canada and the United States. This is saying a lot—Cuba's tuberculosis rate is below those of Canada and the United States.

Plenty could be said about all this, but it would take too long—what is being done, for instance, with German measles, measles, tetanus, and other diseases that have practically disappeared. So our society is getting rid of a series of diseases, which can be done only through a truly sound medical network.

A novel institution, that of the family doctor, was introduced here. We already have more than 6,000 doctors engaged in this type of practice, and in a few years we'll have 20,000 family doctors. The doctors are now starting to be placed in factories, schools, and day-care centers, so we'll have a truly extraordinary medical network.

I think that this year, 1989, we will be graduating 3,600 doctors and by 1990 close to 4,000. More doctors graduate in our country every year than the number of doctors imperialism left us with, because out of the 6,000 we had then they took away 3,000 and left us with 3,000. Today we have more than 31,000 doctors, and when the new class graduates in 1989, we will have around 35,000. And they have been trained well, not just in theory but also in practice, taking part constantly in the country's medical services. Medical services cover the entire country, both urban and rural areas, which is precisely what explains the results I pointed out.

We're developing new fields in medicine. Our country is already doing heart transplants and for a long time it has been doing kidney transplants. We are also beginning to do nerve transplants; we now have a center engaged in developing that activity with rather good prospects. We're also doing ocular microsurgery and are advancing considerably in a series of fields that are part of what we might call sophisticated medicine.

In the social sphere, there's practically no unemployment in our country. Statistically speaking, we do have some unemployed people, which is not because of a lack of jobs, because we still have a shortage of labor power in many places—in agriculture, in the mountains, in reforestation, in construction. Rather it has to do with the preference of some young people for certain kinds of work. But that doesn't mean that there are no jobs available for every young man or woman, independent of the fact that it can't always be the type of job that perhaps they prefer.

Social security covers all the workers in the country, 100 percent. And, of course, one of the most sacred obligations of the state relates to pensions, retirement, and all the other social security benefits extended to families in need of them.

Naturally, the imperialists and reactionaries with their allies the world over try to ignore all the other advances of the revolution. For instance, the revolution has considerably advanced in the scientific field. We now have more than 100 scientific institutions, and there were practically none when the revolution triumphed. Imperialism tries to deny our advances in the country's economic development—in agriculture, industry, and construction.

How could the social accomplishments achieved by our country have come about without economic development? And this in spite of the fact that we must develop our country under very difficult conditions, because for the past thirty years we have had to contend with the imperialist blockade of our country. What other countries are subject to that type of blockade? Very few. With a zealous hatred, the empire forbids even the export of medical equipment to Cuba, not even medicines. Not even an aspirin can be brought to Cuba from the United States. It's a merciless blockade to which very few socialist countries are subject. I believe it's only the People's Republic of Korea, Vietnam, and Cuba. And with Cuba it's a fierce blockade, for the imperialists exert pressure on their allies everywhere not to trade with Cuba, not to grant loans to Cuba, not to transfer technology to Cuba.

Nevertheless, our country's economy has grown during these thirty years at a rate higher than 4 percent a year under the conditions of the blockade. I can give you some figures.

To give you one example, our electrical generating capacity has grown more than eightfold during these thirty years, eightfold! Steel production, which was very low in our country, has grown more than sixteenfold. Cement production has grown fivefold; we used to produce 700,000 tons whereas today we produce more than 3.5 million tons. Our production capacity is even greater, but in certain years the industry didn't get the right kind of maintenance. We're now trying to increase cement production until we reach not less than 4.6 million tons, in line with our economic and social development plans.

Production of fertilizers has grown fivefold. Citrus fruit production has grown seventeenfold. Egg production has grown eightfold, and so on with many other products. Nickel production has doubled and keeps growing. The machine industry is young in our country and is now developing rapidly. More than 6,000 cane harvesters have been manufactured, just to give one example of machine industry production output. To a greater or lesser extent, all our agricultural and industrial production has increased. Our textile industry is another example. Growth has been sustained in all the branches of our economy, in some more and in others less.

The fishing industry, an important source of food, has grown tenfold over these years of the revolution. And it would have grown much more if it hadn't been for an international measure that we supported because it was just, although it didn't benefit us. I'm referring to the 200-mile economic zone.[1] If it hadn't been for this measure that we, as a Third World country, supported, we would have increased our fishing production twenty-five or thirty times over, because we already had a relatively large fishing fleet and the trained personnel for ocean fishing.

These are all real, serious efforts that the country has been making in many fields of the economy and not just in the fields of education, health, and sports. But the empire tries to deny everything. It's in its interest to say that the revolution is not prospering, is not getting anywhere. That's a sort of myth that many people took for fact and so there are many people who speak well of Cuba and say: "They've had great successes in health and in education." The imperialists don't mention the other successes of the revolution, in order to promote the idea that socialism is a failure.

What did our country begin with to tackle its development plans? Our country tackled its development plans with personnel who had barely finished sixth grade. Nearly all our administrators, and a large portion of our engineers, university professors, and technicians went off with their imperialist masters, with the bourgeoisie, with the landowners. We had few agronomists, few veterinarians, and even less stayed, since a large portion left the country. Our country had to start from zero in facing those problems. Sugar mills were often administered by workers who had barely finished sixth grade, and this was how we had to perform during the early years of the revolution.

The revolution lacked experience; it was, so to speak, the first socialist process launched by a Third World country. There wasn't any experience available on how to construct socialism in a Third World country.

Vietnam, a Third World country, had been liberated before we were, but not the whole country, just a part of it, and that country had to concentrate mainly on the liberation struggle. It was our lot to have the experience of building socialism ninety miles from the United States—actually a bit closer, given that we have a Yankee base in Guantánamo, in the eastern region, and no distance separates the Yankee base from our territory—and against a fierce U.S. blockade.

We committed errors—yes, we have committed many errors, and it was to a certain extent understandable for us to commit errors. We committed two types of errors: during one phase we committed errors of idealism and in another phase, while trying to correct our errors of idealism, we committed errors of economism and commercialism. I often use a stronger term and brand them as errors of market mania.

We are now rectifying those errors, and the rectification was very necessary, without falling into previous errors of idealism. We are moving slowly, but results have started to become evident everywhere. This is not easy. Nobody should think it will be easy, since it deals with the theory having to do with the methods and forms of building socialism in a given country. All countries are different; no two are exactly alike. I would say that no two revolutionary processes can be exactly alike.

Our revolution was creative. There was no lack of creative spirit in our revolution; its creative spirit was truly great. For example, the way in which we carried out our agrarian reform was truly creative. The historical precedent was that all countries that started to build socialism divided up the land into small parcels among millions of people and then collectivized little by little, sometimes more or less rapidly or abruptly, sometimes using more political methods and at other times more coercive methods. That never happened in our country. We didn't divide the land at the beginning; the big capitalist enterprises and the big latifundia were maintained as large production units and became state agricultural enterprises.

All the sharecroppers, tenant farmers, squatters, and those who had plots of land were freed from having to pay rent in money or in kind. They were given titles and became small independent farmers. Over the years—after we had given a big push to state enterprises in agriculture, which had the same character as our industries—we slowly and calmly, using political and economic methods, encouraged the independent peasants to join cooperatives.

This process of organizing cooperatives has advanced, although 8 percent of the land is still in the hands of tens of thousands of independent owners.

We didn't have to invent the independent landholder; we didn't have to discover him because we know him and he has been present since the victory of the revolution. He still exists and will remain as long as he wants because we won't compel anyone to join cooperatives by force. We avoid this, and there's not a single instance when anyone has ever been forced to join a cooperative.

But the cooperative movement continues to advance, so that now 80 percent of the land is in state enterprises, 12 percent is in cooperatives, and 8 percent is owned by independent farmers. We assist and cooperate with them, we urge them to produce, and we provide technical support, loans, etc. We write off all loans if there is a disaster, a hurricane, a blight, or something of that sort. But the bulk of the country's agricultural production in key sectors such as sugar, cattle, citrus, rice, meat, milk, and eggs is the result of the work, first of all, of state farms, and secondly, of cooperatives.

State farms and cooperatives provide the great bulk of the country's agricultural products, among them sugar, our chief crop. The 8 percent of land run by small farmers helps, but it does not play a fundamental role in the development of Cuban agriculture. Of course, this agriculture is increasingly better because at first there was the same problem of lack of agronomists, economists, or veterinarians, and the initial state farm administrators had only fifth- or sixth-grade educations.

Our agriculture exports food for 40 million people around the world, 40 million! It exports calories for 40 million people with sugar, citrus fruits, and other crops.

If we had not undertaken the type of agrarian reform we did, it would have meant the end of sugar production as an agricultural industry. We would have fallen into having small plots and production for individual consumption and would not have been able to meet the fundamental needs of the population.

I believe our revolution was creative, for example, when it undertook the campaign against illiteracy; in this it became a model.[2] We were the first country to virtually eradicate illiteracy in a year, utilizing hundreds of thousands of people, basically students. That was the start and then came the follow-up campaigns.

I repeat that the revolution has been creative in a lot of things, and I would say that some of the things we have done were ours alone, not done by other countries, and we are really proud of several of them.

I think, for example, that the study and work system in education is unique. No other country in the world has it. Combining study and work is the application of the ideas of Marx and Martí.

But we didn't just limit ourselves to noting the ideas of Marx and Martí, two great thinkers, two great revolutionaries who raised this idea. At a given stage we decided to implement it because we believed in it, because we were absolutely convinced that if education became universal, work would also have to become universal. Otherwise, future societies would simply become societies of intellectuals unable to work with their hands. And that may be one of the most serious problems faced by the world of the future, especially those seeking a just social system and the construction of socialism.

It is terrible that people should shirk manual labor, and we decided to universalize the practice, first through the School Goes to the Countryside program and then through the schools in the countryside. Thus today virtually everyone under forty years of age has done productive work with their hands. This is a general standard, and I think the excellent qualities of our young people, the thousands of hours of voluntary work they do, the tasks they undertake here or in any part of the world have a lot to do with the system of education established by the Cuban revolution, the system of study and work. [Applause]

Now we have started to see the fruits of this system, every day and everywhere. Nobody here is surprised when asked to work in construction or agriculture. There are truly impressive examples. The largest citrus fruit plantation in the world is here, in Matanzas, about 45,000 hectares [111,000 acres] of fruit trees, which will have over 50,000 a few years from now, or maybe 60,000, on difficult and rocky terrain. It was a sparsely populated area, and the project has been developed utilizing the schools in the countryside with the participation of students who do three hours of work daily. That doesn't hurt anybody; on the contrary, it makes them smarter and teaches them more about life; they learn to appreciate their studies. I only wish I had been educated in a school of this kind!

This year more than 400,000 tons of citrus, worth more than 100 million pesos, have been produced on the Matanzas plantation, with labor based on the schools in the countryside. The sixty schools in the area are the soul of the project.

I urge you to tour the world to see if there is any project like this one, with a production of 400,000 tons—of course, it was started several years ago and is the product of a concept that was starting to come into its own—based on study and work, the efforts of the students, who are proud of it. Production increases every year, and I am sure that one day they will produce a million tons of citrus because the project has already become a scientific and educational complex. They are applying technology—different irrigation systems, fertilization, plant treatment—and they are rapidly making gains. In the last two or three years the project has made a lot of progress.

But that isn't the only one. Those programs exist in nearly all the provinces of the country. That's the largest, but there is also the one on the Isle of Youth. This is one of the basic features of our educational system. And I repeat, it is unique in the world.

We also have voluntary work. In our country voluntary work has reached levels greater than anywhere else in the world. We can safely say so based on the facts, on reality. The participation of the masses in the solution of problems, making a contribution to society, has already become part of the culture of our people. It is part of the thinking and ideology of our revolution, and those levels have not been reached anywhere else. Here it is done systematically.

I think the conception of the minibrigades is another contribution of our revolution that helps to rationalize the work force while promoting mass participation in the social development of the country, because we must build many day-care centers, schools, polyclinics, and especially housing.

We can increase the production of stone, sand, cement. We can do a lot in the manufacturing of materials. But we need people to build all those projects, and often there aren't enough people for the economic and industrial projects because public works construction requires people.

I won't give the guests here an explanation of how the idea of the minibrigades developed around the year 1970, how they were very promising but then declined because of the errors of commercialism and economism I mentioned earlier, and because of certain economic mechanisms that were introduced. These proved to be really sinister; there is no other way to describe it. Now the minibrigades have been revived, in a much better and stronger way. They are the answer to our problems of social development. Not the only one, but one of the most fundamental, especially in the capital of the republic.

Before the rebirth of the minibrigades we couldn't even consider the idea of building a day-care center in the capital simply because we didn't have the workers to build it. One single day-care center or polyclinic! When the minibrigades were reborn in the capital, we built fifty-four day-care centers in one year. Allow me to tell you that the five-year plan had stipulated five. Day-care construction had been totally neglected simply because we didn't have the workers. And then fifty-four were built in one year.

In this past year plus a few days of January—that is, last

year, 1988, and the first days of January—there will be about fifty-six day-care centers. One hundred and ten in two years! At the rate we were going without minibrigades, it would have taken us 100 years to build those day-care centers! The minibrigades were the resounding response to the social development needs of the population: the construction of housing, day-care centers, and schools.

This year, thanks to the work of the minibrigades, the capital will have all the polyclinics it needs. We had them, but some were based in inadequate buildings or those designed for other purposes. Some of the new ones have been finished, and others are under construction; twenty will be finished this year.

This year the minibrigades will finish the twenty-four additional special schools needed in the capital for this branch of education.

I'm not sure if our guests know what the minibrigades are, but it's very simple. Factories or workplaces are asked, "How many workers do you have?" "A thousand." "Send twenty, thirty, forty, fifty, or a hundred." Because in all factories and work centers under both socialism and capitalism—for different reasons that would take too long to explain here—there is excess personnel, be it because of narrow job profiles, paternalism, or an inflated payroll. So we would tell them, "Send fifty and those remaining can do the job." Without working extra hours the others can do the job easily, with a little rationalization. Minibrigade members receive the same wage as in their workplaces, but with a difference: it's said that at their workplace they work forty-four hours a week. I would like to know at what factory the workers really work forty-four hours, making full use of the workday.

Minibrigade members work sixty, sixty-five, or seventy hours a week. Doing what? Building housing for the factory workers and other public works.

Not all the apartments were for the workplace. The state

makes a big contribution. The factory pays wages, and the state repays the factories. The worker gets his factory pay, and the state provides the materials, land, blueprints, and equipment, everything. Factories get 50 percent of the homes they build, and starting this year it will be 60 percent. [*Applause*] A certain percentage must always be at the disposal of the state because there are people who cannot become minibrigade members, teachers for example. It's not easy and there are a lot of needs that arise, so we need a reserve of housing.

But it's very attractive to have the factory send the workers, rationalize itself and cut costs while building housing for the workers at the factory or building other public works I mentioned. This is a very attractive formula. This movement has tremendous power.

Then there are the social minibrigades, which is something else: people build their own homes in previously unhealthy neighborhoods or where there is poor housing. If a housewife joins the minibrigade, she is paid. If a young person who neither studies nor works joins, he or she is paid. If there are workers who are not indispensable at their factories and can be released, they can join. Those are the social minibrigades.

In the capital there are now more than 35,000 minibrigade members. Now the problem is not the work force but materials, and we are hard at work on this in the construction materials industry. But there is no lack of people. In fact, we could almost say we have an excess due to these concepts in which the masses are given the opportunity for concrete and direct participation in solving their problems. If there is no available work force, then who will build the housing? The masses.

And it should be said that ExpoCuba was basically built by the minibrigades. [*Applause*]

What perhaps most impressed the visitors was that it

was not built by professional construction workers. They were amazed to see how a project of this kind could be undertaken.

Without the idea of minibrigades we couldn't even dream of something like this! Before, we would have to send the person who suggested a project like this to the psychiatric hospital immediately, as an urgent case. We didn't have the workers to build one day-care center and this year the minibrigades have built more than fifty, together with many other things, thousands upon thousands of homes, and this giant one, ExpoCuba. They have helped make all sorts of construction materials, the other things, and this giant—for it has really been a gigantic effort—and the minibrigades have done it. That says a lot, and it explains the concept of mass participation.

If there is joy over this project, if we will have something as extraordinarily useful as this national exhibition center, so useful in every sense—including to evaluate the quality of products, to solicit the public's view of industry, to encourage all branches of the economy and services to display their work—it is because of the minibrigades, it is because a mass method to solve important problems emerged. I think that's one of the most notable things about this project.

Perhaps this will give visitors a better idea of what the minibrigades are. There is no need to give Cubans this explanation. They know all about it.

Another concept typical of our revolution is the idea of contingents of construction workers, which is also a unique institution. [*Applause*]

I asked you to excuse me for the positive things we would talk about on this birthday, and I know there are many good things in many parts of the world, in many revolutionary countries. But I will say that there are no groups of construction workers like the contingents that have been organized in our country, based on certain principles and dedication to work. And it didn't start in construction; rather it began at a scientific center.

The construction contingents have yielded fabulous results. The first contingent was created in 1987 as part of the rectification process, and now there are 10,000 to 15,000 construction workers in the contingents and the figure will increase.

The achievements of the first contingent, the Blas Roca Contingent, are really incredible. [*Applause*] The important thing is that the concept has been extended and there are now contingents in every province.

What is a construction contingent? It's a group of workers for whom certain concepts of organization and pay have been established. We apply the socialist formula of pay, according to the quantity and quality of work. There are no other mechanisms, such as those that created a big fuss in construction and terribly affected quality. We sought adequate principles regarding pay, but the first principle is that these workers do what they do not because of what they are paid. No man would do for money what these contingents do. Payment according to work shows society's consideration for their efforts, but they work according to certain principles.

There is no work schedule; the eight-hour day has been forgotten. It may be good in Britain, the Federal Republic of Germany, countries with high productivity, with a lot of machinery, automated lathes, and all that. Because one of the worst things passed on to us by the former colonial or neocolonial rulers were their habits of consumption or their aspirations for consumption and their norms of work, when labor productivity in those countries is far superior. In Cuba after the revolution we often lacked workers, as I told you, because there were not enough for construction or because they didn't like that work.

That doesn't mean we've abolished the eight-hour day. God forbid we should abolish the eight-hour day! They would say we were the most retrograde people on earth.

We have invented something much better: groups of workers who forget about hours. People here work every other Saturday. Previously, people worked every Saturday until noon, and then it was changed to every other Saturday. But all contingents forget about the so-called nonworking Saturdays. [*Applause*] They ignore labor legislation in the sense that labor discipline is not imposed by a law, a judge, or an official of the Ministry of Labor, nor any administrator. In the contingents the workers themselves handle discipline! They are the ones who censure or punish because the contingent won't tolerate laziness or absenteeism. They don't tolerate those who come to work late. It's amazing—there is virtually no absenteeism in the contingents, and the workers handle discipline. The construction contingents are based on dedication to work.

This doesn't mean it will always be like that. This is a stage of struggle for a Third World country that wants to build socialism and develop itself. If we had an excess of people, we of course wouldn't have to do this. We could have three shifts. Contingents work one shift of at least twelve hours, but usually it's fourteen or fifteen hours.

We always have to fight to make sure they don't overdo it in their work. What an interesting phenomenon! Historically there has always been a struggle to have people work hard, and here we have to watch over the contingents and tell them, "Don't overdo it, that's too much, finish at 10:00 and sleep so many hours." They are always inventing a pretext to work—that it rained on such and such a day and they couldn't work so things are behind schedule and they want to finish. We have to fight with them.

The workers in the contingent are the best fed in Cuba. Care for people—a key thing—is the principle. Workers on the contingent have a doctor, direct medical care. They have air conditioning in their rooms. There are no mosquitoes or heat. They have good dormitories, food, and clothing.

The secret is caring for people, which is vital in building socialism. The capitalists, who are neither foolish nor slow, often invent methods of this sort, for they want to exploit the individual, extract more surplus value out of him, so often they provide care for workers.

Under socialism the individual was sometimes forgotten. Since work was a duty, everything was presented as the duty of the worker. So one of the things we've stressed is the importance of giving attention to the individual, of making him see that he's getting the consideration he deserves, that he's given the trust he merits.

We have faith in those things. Had this not been the case where would the revolution have gone? The revolution had to be made under very difficult conditions in the mountains. And in the mountains it became clear what man was capable of doing and becoming.

If you don't trust people, it's better to abandon all claims of being a revolutionary and do something else. If you don't trust people, it's better to abandon all claims of being a socialist and invent something else—which need not be invented for it was already invented long ago.

Capitalism doesn't have to worry about any of these problems. Capitalism was invented by history with spontaneous laws, while socialism must be the product of planned work. It is the first opportunity in history to plan development, and that is an extraordinary privilege.

If you trust in people, you can see the miracles man is capable of, both in the revolutionary struggle to conquer power and in the construction of socialism.

Of course, we didn't know the things we know now. We didn't see them with the clarity we do now. We weren't born revolutionaries, by no means. We have had to learn as we go and every day we learn something new.

In the contingents a new $100,000 bulldozer equals three

of its kind elsewhere. The care and upkeep of equipment and how it's used is really impressive and promising. This is one of the most recent creations of the revolution.

I think the family doctor institution as part of the Cuban concept of primary health care is unique in the world. It was an idea that arose a few years ago. It was put into practice, tested, and then extended. Now there are family doctors in all the mountains of the eastern region of the country, and 63 percent of the population in the capital is now covered by the family doctor program. This concept will be implemented in the day-care centers, schools, and factories. It is one of the incredible results, one of the creations of the revolution, a new concept of the revolution.

We could talk about a lot of other things. I believe our conception and system of broad-based, all-encompassing mass organizations is unique, the way in which it has been done here.

Regarding our electoral system—and the institutions of the revolution are so often called into question—the way delegates are nominated in the electoral districts, which are the foundation for all the state's power, I believe our electoral system is also unique. This is so because the party does not nominate candidates to be delegates, there must be more than one candidate and not more than eight, and they are nominated by the people without any participation by the party. The party doesn't say we nominate this candidate or that one; it is the people who do the nominating. That doesn't exist in any other country.

In the face of the impudent slanders against our revolution, we don't have to feel ashamed if we have an electoral system that no other country has. And it was established because the revolution emerged and developed closely linked to the masses.

If the people were counterrevolutionary, if the majority of the people were counterrevolutionary, all they need do would be to nominate counterrevolutionaries and the majority of the delegates would be counterrevolutionaries opposed to the revolution and socialism. Every five years we have two grass-roots elections and delegates can be recalled by the voters.

The electoral system established by the Cuban revolution is unique! We don't have to go anywhere to learn anything. Rather we could say, come here to learn how a democratic electoral system functions. [Applause]

There is something else associated with this. I believe our conception of defense is unique, the way it has developed, with the total participation of the masses. Other countries have very good things, I wouldn't deny it, there are others. But we feel we have our own form and conception of how to organize defense with the participation of the entire people—workers, students, men and women, so that millions are actively involved in our defense.

To some of the Western countries that question democracy in Cuba we can say: there can be no democracy superior to that where the workers, the peasants, and the students have the weapons. They have the weapons! [Applause] To all those Western countries that question democracy in Cuba we can say: give weapons to the workers, give weapons to the peasants, give weapons to the students, and we'll see whether tear gas will be hurled against workers on strike, against any organization that struggles for peace, against the students; [Applause] we'll see whether the police can be ordered to attack them while wearing masks and all those contrivances that make them look like space travelers; [Laughter] we'll see whether the dogs can be turned loose on the masses every time there's a strike or a peace demonstration or a people's struggle.

I believe that the supreme test of democracy is arming the people! [Applause] When defense becomes the task of the entire people and weapons become the prerogative of the entire people, then they can talk about democracy. Until then they can talk about specialized police forces and armies to crush the people whenever the people protest against the abuses and injustices of the bourgeois system, whether in a Third World capitalist country or in a developed capitalist country.

What do we see constantly on television? What do we see on the news broadcasts from the United States, from Europe—the same Europe that boasts so much about its democratic institutions? What we see is the people being trampled upon at the hands of experts in repression and brutality, something that has never been seen during these thirty years of revolution in our country. And I believe these are characteristics typical of our revolution.

I would daresay—and it would pain me if anybody feels hurt by this—that the level of massive internationalist consciousness achieved by our people has never been achieved by any other country. [*Applause*] And we have proof of this every day, not just from statistics—more than 300,000 of our compatriots have fulfilled internationalist missions in Angola through our Revolutionary Armed Forces. [*Prolonged applause*] That does not include civilian workers. It is shown by the fact that at this moment there are 50,000 of our compatriots in Angola and something still more important: if 50,000 additional fighters would have been needed, our people would have been capable of sending them! [*Applause*]

Proof can be found in the fact that when 2,000 teachers were needed for Nicaragua, 30,000 stepped forward, and when the contras murdered a number of Cuban teachers, 100,000 stepped forward, practically all the primary school teachers in our country. [*Applause*]

Proof can be found in the fact that when an earthquake hit Peru, more than 100,000 blood donations were made throughout the country in ten days, ten days! [*Applause*] And proof can be found in the fact that in the wake of the

Armenian earthquake more than 30,000 Cubans—just from the capital alone, mind you, not the whole country—donated their blood. [*Applause*] And I saw the spirit with which our compatriots from the capital were determined to make hundreds of thousands of donations if that were needed, just from the capital.

We tried to do everything in a highly organized way so that not a single drop of blood would be lost, so that it could be processed properly, and the period of donations was limited since no more blood was needed, but the capital could have easily made 50,000, 60,000 donations, which is equivalent—if the whole country had donated—to 250,000 blood donations. That's the kind of spirit we saw!

We normally have 400,000, 500,000 donations a year, but our people are capable of donating that much in a month if we had the facilities to collect it, store it, and process it. I think that is an extraordinary proof of internationalism.

I saw the proof every day I would go visit this or that workplace and I found out that everybody's question was, "Listen, count on me. Listen, I'm not on the list yet. Listen, we want to go repair the damage caused by the hurricane in Nicaragua. We want to go to Armenia."

Our problem whenever we meet a group of workers is that they are constantly asking us for the honor of going to help rebuild Bluefields [Nicaragua] or going to help rebuild Armenia.

I believe the internationalist spirit of our people has reached extremely high levels, and we can feel proud of this.

Was it like that before? In a bourgeois society can anyone find a young man who says: "Listen, I want to go to Bluefields. Listen, I want to go to Armenia to build. Listen, I want to go on a mission to support the people of Angola or any other people." That was nowhere to be seen. It's inconceivable. It's inconceivable in a bourgeois society where man is alienated, where moral and ethical values practically don't count at all. Yet volunteering for an internationalist mission is a common thing among our workers, among our young people.

I think that our people's spirit of collaboration with Third World countries does not exist in any other Third World country. A country like Cuba, struggling for development, has reached extremely high levels in international collaboration, too. Our doctors are in dozens of countries, our construction workers, our teachers are there donating their services.

We're also the country with the highest number of foreign students per capita. On the Isle of Youth alone there are more than 18,000 foreign students. I think that's also a unique, extraordinary experience linking our people with the rest of the world.

That is what characterizes the spirit of our revolution and the creations of our revolution. That is what gives us so much satisfaction and that is what we should trust. And we must carry on with that creative spirit, with this noble undertaking of building socialism in our country.

Speaking of this, I had almost forgotten to speak about ExpoCuba. Not only had I forgotten about ExpoCuba but also about the Botanical Gardens. We had agreed to inaugurate the Botanical Gardens today as well. We're now in the middle with the Botanical Gardens on one side of us and ExpoCuba on the other.

Establishing the Botanical Gardens took many years, twenty years. Naturally the Botanical Gardens had to be created by planting many tiny plants, many of them seedlings. At times we grew impatient and said, "Can't trees be transplanted?" But the experts replied, "Seedlings grow to be more resistant than transplanted trees." Anyway, we have there a number of transplanted trees because we had no other choice, certain types of palm trees, and so on.

It has taken twenty years to create the Botanical Gardens! It covers 600 hectares. I think it's an extraordinary scientific center, a task for which, from a scientific viewpoint, the University of Havana, its biology branch, was responsible. Today it has become a reality, twenty years after work began to build it, and it's already in operation. We had to inaugurate it someday and I think this is the day. ExpoCuba over here and the Botanical Gardens over there. The main installations have been completed. Always in these centers there's something to be built, to be added, new needs spring up. But now the Botanical Gardens are a reality as real as ExpoCuba, with the difference that in the Botanical Gardens the trees are green and in ExpoCuba the trees have yet to turn green, because the landscaping has just been completed and it will take a few more weeks for them to turn green.

That's why we had decided to inaugurate these two institutions today to mark the thirtieth anniversary.

We must recall here the cooperation given us by a German scientist, a true disciple of Alexander von Humboldt,[3] Professor Bisse, who helped us draw up the concept of the Botanical Gardens. Unfortunately, four years ago while working in our country, Professor Bisse was killed in a traffic accident. Nevertheless, he left us a legacy of many of his ideas, his conception of these Botanical Gardens.

Some compañeros spoke here today about ExpoCuba before I did. Its director mentioned very interesting facts and so did the compañero in charge of its construction. I've already pointed out this was a project of the minibrigades.

If anything else remains to be said, it would be that from the standpoint of construction this project was a true learning process. The practical methods used, the savings in materials, the use of lightweight steel for the sections, all this offers us a construction method that can be used to speed up many projects, given that the construction technique utilized here can be applied to building warehouses, supermarkets, and other projects.

Already in Santiago de Cuba there are plans to use the

same technique in the railroad station so that it can be finished before the Fourth Congress of the Communist Party of Cuba. On the basis of these experiences we can solve countless other problems using the same construction technique.

I have to say that normally buildings with steel beam construction weigh sixty kilograms [132 pounds] per square meter and these weigh twenty.

It should be said that the draftsmen, technicians, designers, all of them Cuban, who planned the project on the basis of a given idea have, in my opinion, really covered themselves with glory, because they have made it functional and beautiful. They took the idea given them about what we wanted and developed it, or rather they extended it, and achieved truly impressive results. This is a point worthy of being singled out—the work done by the draftsmen, architects, engineers, and designers.

Another thing worthy of being singled out was the spirit of cooperation. More than 100 different enterprises worked together to complete ExpoCuba.

There was outstanding support by all the agencies involved in the project because they were committed to the simple idea of having a pavilion to exhibit their wares.

As I was saying a few days ago at a meeting with the Expo-Cuba workers and those who built it, I had often visited this place but I hadn't discovered ExpoCuba. It was just recently, on a day when I was riding around all the buildings, that I realized how gigantic the project is.

I think it has been a great accomplishment, enormously useful, and that the experiences we can derive from this will be very important for our economy, not just through the exhibits but also through the experience gained in building ExpoCuba.

The project was completed truly in record time. From the moment the idea emerged and was explained to a group of compañeros who were given the job of building it, until the moment it was completed, hardly twenty-four months have passed. Throughout all that period the plans were drawn up, the draftsmen worked at the construction site, the earth-moving operations began twenty months ago, and without many resources or much labor power. The project really got going barely a year ago, in December 1987, and they have accomplished the feat of finishing it a few hours prior to this ceremony. We could say that ExpoCuba was completed early this morning. [*Applause*]

I was here just five days ago, and they still had many sidewalks, staircases, and a string of other things to finish. The essential and fundamental things are now finished.

Whenever visitors came, the first thing they asked was whether this was going to be finished. And I recall that one day when I was with the construction workers, I was talking with the same compañero who wrote the hymn. Just as I was about to ask whether the project would be finished by January 1, he suddenly said to me, "We have here some verses entitled 'Yes, it will be finished,' which we recite to everybody who comes here and pesters us, asking whether it will be finished." [*Applause*] I was lucky they showed me the verses before I asked whether the project would be finished on time!

Naturally, I was confident that they were indeed going to finish it, because I know what people can do when they are determined, when a person applies himself, when a person proposes to do something.

The work shift here lasted fourteen, fifteen hours, sometimes more, and there were many occasions when the workers stayed at the job during two consecutive shifts, twenty-four hours and even thirty hours. Those were the hours of voluntary work that they did after putting in eight hours of work, plus the hours they put in on nonworking Saturdays and on Sundays. That's impressive!

I recall being introduced to Compañero Avelino during one of my visits here. I was told he was going to put in I-don't-know-how-many hours of voluntary work, and he did it. How many hours was it? [*People answer: "3,500!"*] Thirty-five hundred hours of voluntary work! Many more voluntary hours than those one would work in an ordinary shift for an entire year. Every time I came here I bumped into him, and at times his eyes were red from working so hard.

It's that sort of thing we would not want them to do, but who can stop them, who's going to prohibit them? No one pushed him into it. No one appealed to him or asked him to do it. It was his own decision when he said, "I'm going to do so many thousands of hours."

On many occasions I came at night or in the early morning and I always saw him there, with reddened eyes, as I said, and I wondered how this compañero could withstand it. And here he is now. He was the first to get his certificate for 3,500 voluntary hours, and looking younger than ever. [*Applause*]

While giving out the certificates, I was impressed when some of them told me: "I'm already on the list of those going to Bluefields," or else, "I'm not on the list and I want to be included on the list to go to Bluefields." I already told them that not everybody would be able to go to either Bluefields or Armenia—about Armenia the Soviets still have to decide if they are going to accept cooperation workers from other countries to help with the reconstruction.

The aid to reconstruct Bluefields has already been agreed upon with Nicaragua, and I think that within a few days they'll be working there. I repeat that, naturally, not everybody can go to Bluefields or to Armenia.

When I was talking about the internationalist spirit of our people I should have mentioned that 300,000 construction workers volunteered to help reconstruct Armenia. That's a truly impressive figure. [*Applause*] Of course we can't send 300,000 there, nor 30,000 or 10,000. It will rather have to be symbolic in one sense, although an effective contribution.

Perhaps 1,000, 2,000, maybe even 3,000. We could do it provided the Soviets decide to accept them. But the important thing is that 300,000 stepped forward.

If there's anything left to be said about this project it's that anyone touring it in its entirety—and he'd have to walk for kilometers—if he was told that the country has invested there $50 million in parts imported from capitalist countries, he would think it logical, normal. However, in this project, where the bookkeeping was kept down to the last penny for everything that was bought—whether it be the raw materials for some paints, or photographic materials, or electrical materials, or materials of different kinds, or some motor of a type we don't have, or some kinds of lamps we don't have—the investment was $5.6 million in convertible currency, in today's dollars, which are worth practically nothing. It's really incredible when you see the results. They're making precise estimates on all the materials obtained from socialist countries, what the cost was—not the cost of finished products, as the enterprises figure it now, but the cost of the raw materials, above all the steel from the socialist countries, mainly the USSR, and we think it won't exceed 7 or 8 million rubles.

If anybody were told that this project would cost $150 million, he would accept it without much fuss. I'm certain that in the United States this project would cost not less than $150 million, excluding the land, which inflates the cost of projects there.

The project has cost roughly 30 million pesos. And if we keep in mind that it was built by minibrigade members, the salary component could be deducted, which means that building the project did not involve a single cent of additional expenses, in the main. Naturally, some state agencies helped with the construction, but using workers from those same agencies. It was not additional labor power hired to do construction work.

I think that even the convertible currency expenses can be recovered in less than three years, inasmuch as we think that future international fairs scheduled for Havana can and should be staged in this national exhibition center to help recover the convertible currency expenses in a short time by leasing the premises to foreign enterprises. I think that the workers here have really accomplished a feat worthy of the thirtieth anniversary.

I'm aware that I've taken a long time to say all this. However, there are still a few more things I should not fail to mention today, especially of an international nature. [*Applause*]

It would be very difficult to fail to link this thirtieth anniversary with the peace accords for southwestern Africa.

I already spoke on December 5 about the factors that led to the recent effort made by our country in Angola, the critical situation that had developed there, the need to save that situation. I explained all that and I shouldn't repeat it now.

You will recall, too, how we said that any peace accord would have to be made on the basis of principles, and that if it wasn't on the basis of principles, there would be no peace accords. We said very clearly, in the face of certain demands by the South African racists, that there would be no accord if we had to comply with certain demands and that, if necessary, we were prepared to remain there ten, fifteen, or twenty more years. In all this we were acting in close coordination with the government of the People's Republic of Angola.

Finally, the last obstacles were overcome and the agreements were signed along the lines you know. I believe this also was an extraordinary victory for our people's internationalist spirit.

But this is not the time for singing praise for what was done. This is a historical task that ought to be written down someday in all its details. What matters now is the fact that those accords were reached and were signed at the United Nations.

Now comes a very important part of this process, which is the implementation of UN Resolution 435, adopted more than ten years ago. This is a fundamental question, for it has to do with the question of the independence of Namibia, for which tens of thousands of SWAPO [South West Africa People's Organisation] fighters have fought and sacrificed their lives over many years.

It is now in order to create all the conditions so an election can be held in an independent Namibia to decide its fate. And we are all aware of the vast support that the Namibian independence fighters understandably have among the people.

However, certain obstacles have now arisen. And on this subject so as not to leave anything to improvising and in order to say everything with precision and clarity, I brought here some papers that I wish to read.

It is necessary for our people and international opinion to be clearly aware of the difficulties that have arisen due to certain attempts at modifying UN Security Council Resolution 435. The idea of making such modifications stems from the United States, a permanent member of that council.

During the course of the four-party negotiations, our delegation spoke very early on about the need to have the UN Security Council guarantee all the accords that were reached and that the UN should become the guarantor of their fulfillment.

Following the signing of the three-party accords between Angola, Cuba, and South Africa, and the two-party accord between Angola and Cuba, the group of countries belonging to the Movement of Nonaligned Countries that were also at the time sitting on the Security Council, submitted a draft resolution for that purpose. This was independent of another resolution that the council must also approve, specifically referring to the steps that must be taken now to comply with the original resolution regulating the process of Namibian independence, Resolution 435, which was approved more than ten years ago in September 1978.

The Security Council, as you know, is made up of fifteen members, of which five are permanent and ten are rotated and elected by all the other countries.

Simultaneously with this proposal by a group of Third World countries that included six Nonaligned nations plus Brazil, the five UN Security Council permanent members—the United States, the Soviet Union, France, China, and Britain—presented to the council another draft resolution. It makes reference to the accords, but at the same time introduces considerations that represent modifications of the plan for implementing Resolution 435; for that reason they were rejected by the group of Nonaligned countries belonging to the council. These countries are Yugoslavia, Nepal, Senegal, Algeria, Argentina, and Zambia. The latter two are being replaced in January by Colombia and Ethiopia.

The essence of the proposal of the five permanent members is the need to reduce the cost of the Namibian independence process, on grounds, it is claimed, that the estimates were made ten years ago and that at present, apart from the inflation afflicting the world economy, which makes the sum bigger, the UN is facing financial difficulties. It is similarly claimed that the signing of the accords in itself has created favorable conditions allowing for reduced costs through the dispatch of fewer international battalions than what was calculated in great detail in Resolution 435.

It must be said that the approval of these resolutions is a key step in the dynamic begun by the four-party negotiation process, for it is precisely through this approval that the UN secretary-general will be empowered by the Security Council to begin the decolonization of Namibia and lead that country to independence.

Cuba shares the concern of the members of the Nonaligned Movement inside the Security Council, because any consideration of a financial nature must take into account, above all, the political consequences that may derive from this.

It must be remembered that Resolution 435 of 1978 has become the essential element that specifies how Namibia will gain independence.

At the time it was first approved, this resolution was the result of the concerted action of a group of Western countries including the United States. Therefore, it can hardly be judged as partial to the interests of the SWAPO fighters, or as having failed to take into account the demands then made by South Africa, with which discussions were held in detail during the process of drafting the resolution more than ten years ago. After the resolution was ignored by the South African government, the first real possibility is now at hand to implement it, thanks to the peace process to which Angola and Cuba have contributed in a major way.

The international forces that should be arriving in Namibia have an irreplaceable function in the steps foreseen for independence. It is up to them to supervise the cease-fire, assign the South African troops and the SWAPO forces to specific areas, supervise the withdrawal of South African troops and prevent infiltration along Namibia's borders, as well as watch over the dismantling of all local troops set up by South Africa over seven decades of colonial domination.

For its part, the civilian component of the United Nations Transition Assistance Group in Namibia must play an indispensable role in supervising more than 400 polling places for the elections over a territory of more than 800,000 square kilometers.

These calculations made ten years ago took into account the Namibian population existing at the time, which has grown by 50 percent over this period, just as the number of voters who will decide who is to rule the country after the South African withdrawal has also constantly increased.

In 1978, seven battalions of UN troops were estimated

as necessary for all these functions. They must control the pullback of several tens of thousands of South African troops amounting to more than twice the number present ten years ago. The forces of the territorial army, Namibians dependent on South Africa, are estimated at more than 20,000 men. And the police, also trained by the South Africans, today number more than 8,000 men, which is many times larger than the figure when Resolution 435 was adopted.

On the other hand, the rationale that the accords allow for a reduction in the number of men at the border with Angola is also unrealistic, for this zone has never been considered a destabilizing factor for the Namibian independence process. Instead, the area that was always regarded as requiring extreme vigilance during the election process and during the formation of an independent government was precisely the border between Namibia and South Africa, the country which for seventy-three years colonized that territory.

A danger that exists during this delicate transition period is the operations of paramilitary groups that South Africa could organize with members of the so-called Namibian territorial forces, who contributed to the colonization of their own people. The presence of the international forces sent by the UN is the only guarantee for the holding of elections, for which the South African regime has over a number of years been creating favorable conditions for sectors inclined to its colonial and neocolonial interests.

We can't pretend to ignore the important role these international military and civilian forces will play in the process leading up to independence, in creating a favorable psychological climate, in giving confidence to a people subjected to the most brutal forms of colonialism for seven decades.

We are not opposed to efforts to cut costs in implementing Resolution 435, if possible; but there must be no change in its basic aims. There can be no reduction that affects what the UN forces should represent in controlling the withdrawal of the South African army, dissolving the puppet army, bringing the police force under control and reducing it, protecting the people, organizing the return to their country of more than 80,000 Namibian refugees, and creating a climate that will facilitate fair elections, the formation of a government, and independence.

This is what is being debated in New York now: Whether the letter and spirit of the Namibian independence agreements are to be respected or whether—allegedly to cut costs—the right of the Namibian people to self-determination is jeopardized.

Cuba has stated its views on this delicate issue to the government of the Soviet Union and also to China, France, and Britain. In New York, during the final rounds of negotiations, we also explained our views to the U.S. representatives.

The United States is the main sponsor of these reductions, under the pretext of cutting costs. We feel this is not just another agreement, not just another resolution or document, or a new statement. What is at stake is infinitely more important, something for which thousands of Namibian fighters have given their lives, for which Angolan support contributed to Namibian liberation, and for which Cubans have also shed their blood over the last thirteen years of confrontations with the arrogant South Africans in Angola.

What is now at stake is whether or not the mechanisms of the United Nations will be capable of facilitating the expression of the legitimate will of the Namibian people; of assuring the virtually unanimous aspirations of the international community surrounding the peace process in southwestern Africa.

This discussion cannot be treated as simply a financial issue. The United States, which is a cosponsor of Resolution 435, knows very well that any reduction of international troops benefits South Africa.

In this current battle Cuba will maintain its principled

positions as it did during the difficult months of negotiations with South Africa and the United States.

Our country is not a member of the Security Council,
but it is deeply committed to the cause of Namibian independence and to strict respect for the instrument created for
this purpose, that is, Resolution 435. And it is committed
to the position of the Movement of Nonaligned Countries,
clearly expressed by seven of its members who have seats
on the Security Council.

We also believe that in a period such as this, when it seems
that at least in some regions there are chances for negotiated
solutions—which, of course, are only possible through the
tenacious struggle of the peoples—the prestige and authority of the UN must be upheld as never before. This is a responsibility we all have, especially the permanent members
of the Security Council.

What I have read is the essence of the question, and it is
very important, so that the efforts of the Namibians and
other peoples over so many years won't be frustrated.

There is one circumstance in this dispute that could be
considered new. For the first time in the history of the United
Nations, there is a clash of views between the permanent
members of the Security Council—with strong U.S. influence—and the views of the Third World—in this case rep-
resented by the Movement of Nonaligned Countries—on a
matter of great importance to the peoples of the Third World,
related in general to the struggle against apartheid, and in
particular to the elimination of the last vestiges of colonialism and the sovereignty of a country such as Namibia.

This unique and unprecedented event raises the issue—
and I say so with a deep sense of responsibility, because
we are very concerned about what is happening on this
problem—the delicate question of democratization of the
United Nations.

Sometimes there are things that are so sacred, so imposed

by habit and custom, that they seem untouchable. But it seems the time has come to deal with this problem. Otherwise, the development of new conceptions of international relations is out of the question.

We have the right to ask what sort of democracy exists in the United Nations if what is left of the old British empire, which for centuries ruled over much of the world on all continents—Britain, with a population of 50 million inhabitants—has the right to veto Security Council resolutions while a country such as India—to mention just one—with 750 million inhabitants, fifteen times the population of Britain and a former British colony, does not have that right.

We could mention other countries of great economic and industrial importance in the world, or with large populations, or with authority in the United Nations, who do not have that prerogative. In the Third World there are countries such as Brazil, Mexico, and Nigeria, to mention only some with larger populations and more territory than Britain.

The Third World as a whole has a population of not less than four billion people and their most sacred interests, aspirations, or hopes can be frustrated simply by the veto of any of the five permanent members of the Security Council. The United States has made use of this privilege countless times.

Nearly half a century has passed since the end of World War II, and we live in a diametrically different world that must have different norms. And now we see that four billion human beings of the part of the world that was colonized, exploited, enslaved, and bled dry have no rights of this sort at all. I believe this is a very important issue that we should think about, and it is our duty to sincerely raise the issue at this time, when we witness a new experience as a result of the dispute in the Security Council regarding Resolution 435. I think it is a question that Cuban and especially world public opinion should closely follow.

We have exhausted all our means—talks, contacts, and argument with the members of the Security Council and so far the desired results apparently have not been achieved. There can be many ways to cut costs. African countries that are closer to Namibia than countries on other continents could be asked to help. I'm sure that many African countries would be willing, at minimal expense, to maintain the indispensable number of battalions in Namibia. There are many ways to cut costs, and we aren't opposed to that aim. It's too bad we can't be there, because we could send the seven battalions and not charge a cent. [*Applause*] But under the circumstances we can't because we are a party to the conflict.

But there are countries such as Nigeria, Ethiopia, and Tanzania, there are many countries of Africa that would gladly cooperate at minimal expense, reducing the cost of transportation and spending of all sorts. Getting seven battalions together is not so difficult.

At first the United States was floating the idea of reducing it from seven to three battalions—something really alarming—and now we have this problem in the Security Council, which we are of course duty bound to explain, for everyone will have to assume the corresponding responsibility if the South Africans are able in any way to frustrate Namibia's right to independence, using fraud, pressure, or terror to impose a puppet government.

We hope the problem will be solved, that there won't be arrogance or high-handedness on the part of permanent members of the Security Council and that a reasonable and just formula will be found, discussed out with the representatives of the Movement of Nonaligned Countries and the Third World on the Security Council.

We have worked in a very serious manner, with the hope that these problems can be solved, and we are taking steps to strictly abide by the agreements signed at the Security Council in New York.

It is our responsibility to withdraw 3,000 soldiers between the signing of the agreement and April 1, when implementation of Resolution 435 begins. We have three full months for this withdrawal. It was a commitment made as a gesture of goodwill. Cuba and Angola asked the United Nations to confirm the withdrawal of our forces in the agreed-upon period. Therefore, on the tenth of this month the withdrawal of the 3,000 men will start. [*Applause*] The first Cuban internationalist fighters should arrive from Angola on January 11. [*Applause*] This will be a net withdrawal, and all the details have been discussed. The total period will cover twenty-seven months beginning April 1 for the gradual and total withdrawal of our forces. Of course during this time we will have to rotate part of the personnel.

In the case of the 3,000 men, this is a net withdrawal of troops. As far as we are concerned, we will strictly comply with the agreements and we hope others will do likewise.

There is another aspect of international politics I would like to cover briefly. On December 5, as you know, in commemorating the anniversary of the *Granma* landing and the granting of the Banner of Defense Readiness to the capital, addressing hundreds of thousands of combatants we discussed concepts related to defense and the need to always stay alert and to always be ready to defend the country.

We must say something in a clear and sincere manner: we fully support the peace policy of the Soviet Union. This must be made clear because often the imperialist and capitalist press in the Western countries keeps on probing and trying to develop differences between Cuba and the USSR. Or they stress contradictions or exaggerate differences that can and do exist in the forms of rectification and carrying forward the process of socialism, which need not become a source of friction in our relations with the Soviet Union.

I think we must start from the principle of absolute respect for the paths that each country follows or decides to follow in building socialism. But there should not be the slightest doubt that we fully support the peace policy of the Soviet Union. [*Applause*] Not only do we support it, we keenly appreciate it. We are conscious of the importance of preventing nuclear war and halting the arms race. We are conscious of the importance of having a policy of peace prevail in the world, a policy of détente and peaceful coexistence between states with different social systems.

This is vital for the countries of the Third World, for the billions of human beings I mentioned, who suffer deeply from the consequences of poverty and underdevelopment inherited from colonialism. As I said on December 5, in these countries 120,000 children die every three days who could have been saved, which is equivalent to an atomic bomb exploding in their midst every three days. For these countries, burdened by debt and ruthlessly exploited by unequal terms of trade, who so desperately need a new international economic order, halting the arms race and achieving détente, coexistence, and peace are indispensable. Without it there will not be the slightest hope of dealing with problems such as the debt, eliminating the debt, having resources for development, ending unequal terms of trade, and living in an economically more just world. Only the incredible sums spent on the arms race can provide the resources for obtaining those goals.

For us it is of great historic and strategic importance that Comrade Gorbachev spoke at the United Nations upholding these Third World banners and endorsing the goals for which we have been struggling over many years. We say the debt should be canceled; Comrade Gorbachev spoke of a 100-year moratorium. In practice, postponing payment for 100 years is the same as writing it off. [*Applause*]

Linking the objectives of disarmament with development and the need for a new international economic order—these are key and very serious issues linked to peace with which we totally agree and fully support. Who could oppose a policy of peace?

Soviet policy has made itself felt on the international scene with a new climate. It has categorically and unquestionably demonstrated who are the friends and defenders of peace and disarmament. In the vanguard of these defenders we find the socialist countries and the Soviet Union in particular, and this has been demonstrated more clearly than ever before.

Now then, regardless of the great gains that have been achieved, I warned that there was a risk, that there was a very important issue to define: how is peace to be understood, what do the imperialists interpret as peace, and what do they interpret as peaceful coexistence. We expressed our fears that the imperialists, as they have done so often before, will apply their peculiar conception of peace whereby peace is understood as being between the big powers, while at the same time they reserve the right to oppress, exploit, threaten, and attack the countries of the Third World. One day it could be Nicaragua, another Cuba or any other Third World nation, as has happened over the years.

If the imperialists interpret peace to mean the right to apply their policy of being the world's policeman, it is a matter of vital importance for these peoples, and it must be clearly and categorically defined.

Less than thirty days have passed since I made that speech and we already have an example.

In the last few days the United States has made a big uproar over an alleged chemical weapons plant in Libya, and the president of the United States openly mentioned the possibility of launching an air attack on that plant. A U.S. naval squad moved into the Mediterranean after those threatening declarations, and there is a hysterical campaign in the United States intended to create the conditions for the attack. The Libyans have said there is no such chemical weapons plant nor any plans to build one. They are building a medicine plant. But I think even that explanation was unnecessary. Of course, we are not advocates of chemical weapons. We advocate the total elimination of all chemical weapons. But what's at stake here is the right of the United States to determine who may or may not manufacture chemical weapons, to decide that if a country manufactures chemical weapons it will be attacked and bombed. [*Applause*]

The United States has the largest chemical weapons arsenal, a powerful chemical weapons industry, and it feels it has the right to manufacture and stockpile chemical weapons. So how can it deny that right to any other country as long as there is no international agreement to eliminate chemical weapons and ban their production?

Even if Libya were in fact manufacturing chemical weapons, what right does the United States have to bomb that country? What right does it have to bomb that factory? Will the law of the jungle prevail in the world, the law of the strongest? Is that how the United States understands peace and détente? What security can there be for any Third World country under those circumstances?

Now a squadron is advancing toward the Mediterranean, and U.S. television has even explained the technique the Pentagon will use. So that they won't even have to risk planes and ask for overflight rights from other countries, they will launch cruise missiles from a submarine in the Mediterranean. In other words, modern technology at the service of bellicose aggression and threats against the peoples, war against the peoples of the Third World. It is shameful and repugnant, really outrageous, to see how they discuss what type of technology to use for their crimes.

Therefore, we can ask ourselves, what do the imperialists understand by peace?

We want peace and must strive for it. But we want a peace for all peoples, a peace with rights for all the peoples of the world! [*Prolonged applause and shouts of "For sure, Fidel, give the Yankees hell!"*]

Peace with respect, peace with rights, peace with independence, peace with security for all peoples of the world, that's what we must fight for!

These are the definitions that international public opinion demands. I think that now more than ever there must be a very clear international awareness on this question.

There is a lot I could say about these topics. We could even mention the fact that today, in particular, the propaganda and disinformation organs of imperialism—as we could call them—are focused on Cuba. They have singled us out in particular; I don't know what rare privilege we seem to have. In the West they'd like to tell us what to do. We should do this or that, we shouldn't do this or that, we should imitate this, we should copy or not copy that. They have turned this matter, a basic right of our people, into a subject of almost daily discussion.

Of course, none of this scares us or affects our morale. On the contrary, it's a great honor, for we never felt we deserved such attention. We really don't want to give anybody sleepless nights and we don't understand why we're such a source of concern to so many people.

What I can assure you, as I did in Santiago de Cuba on January 1, is that the revolution is not going to change. I think the secret of this revolution is having been loyal to principles from start to finish, having been loyal for thirty years and being willing to continue that way for another thirty or hundred years. [*Applause*]

I think this is the most important legacy we can leave for the new generations: The essential idea that one must be loyal to principles, that there is only one honorable way to survive under conditions as difficult as those Cuba has had to face over the last thirty years; loyalty to principles and never letting yourself be intimidated by anything, not letting anything or anybody change the pure and straight line of the revolution. [*Applause*]

That's what we can offer our friends all over the world. Cuba will remain loyal, it will remain true to those principles. We feel duty bound to say so here because—as I said at the start—this is not just our own work; it is the work of all.

In Santiago de Cuba I explained that the revolution was not just the result of our struggle against Batista. It was the result and the fruit of more than 100 years of struggle by our people, of struggle by many generations ever since national feelings developed in our country.

The same can be said for our socialist revolution. It is not just the product of our own efforts. It is the fruit of centuries of struggle by the peoples, the efforts of the working class since the last century, the fruit of the Paris Commune although it wasn't victorious, the fruit of the October revolution, the fruit of the struggle of all peoples to create a world without slavery and exploitation of man by man, a world of true justice.

A socialist revolution does not occur on a solitary planet. It happens in the world today where there are still great tragedies, where there is still an empire as powerful as the United States, where imperialism is still a reality, and where there is still a group of industrialized capitalist nations who are rich and powerful and impose their selfish standards on much of the world.

Our revolution is the fruit of international cooperation from all the socialist countries and especially the Soviet Union. [*Applause*] We will never forget the support received at key moments when we did not lack the weapons needed for our defense. We will never forget the economic cooperation, the just trade relations established with us by the most developed socialist countries, and especially those between the Soviet Union and Cuba.

The capitalists never tire of saying that this is a donation or subsidy for the Cuban revolution. The things for which Third World nations have been fighting for decades, the just trade we have demanded so as not to be victims of the brutal drama of unequal terms of trade—the mechanism utilized by the developed capitalist countries to sell their products at ever higher prices and to buy our exports at ever cheaper ones—this does not exist in the type of relations we have with the USSR and other socialist countries. Instead, there is a rational and just exchange, as should be the case, between developed and developing countries, even more just within a socialist community. The imperialists call that a subsidy, and you see it printed daily in all the dispatches. The fact that our sugar is bought at a different price and not at the junk level of the world market, where not a lot of sugar is sold, is something they view as a donation. The capitalist countries view this as a precedent that must be fought, because its universal application would mean the end of one of the most repugnant forms of exploitation in the world today.

We will never forget the fact that between the other socialist countries and Cuba, between the Soviet Union and Cuba, it was possible to establish a new type of economic relationship that has made a great contribution to our development efforts and has been very significant in the battles and great successes obtained in many fields. We never imagined that our people alone deserved credit for this; on the contrary, we said our people had to make an ever greater effort, be ever more efficient. And as we attempted to do this, we said that our people had to convert every year into three or four. And I really think we are on that path.

But we could never forget what we have received from the world, what we have received from other peoples. We could never forget the moral and political support and solidarity we have received from all over the world: in Latin America, Asia, and Africa; by progressive, democratic, and revolutionary forces all over the world; and in the capitalist countries themselves, where we have many friends who haven't fallen prey to the abusive and massive propaganda against our revolution.

Therefore at this ceremony and at this moment, on our thirtieth anniversary, the most important and essential thing that remains to be expressed is our gratitude to all of you, those who have been with us on this thirtieth anniversary, gratitude for what you represent, the just causes and noble ideas you express and symbolize.

On behalf of our people, we thank the hundreds of guests present here and their peoples!

Patria o muerte!

Venceremos! [*Ovation*]

TERRY COGGAN

BRIDGET ELTON

Above, members of a minibrigade building a new apartment building in Havana. Below, Cuban internationalist brigade in Bluefields, Nicaragua, helping to rebuild after devastating hurricane.

GEORGE JOHNSON

PRENSA LATINA

Above, billboard in Havana: "Our youth will build communism and forge a new world." Below, members of the Territorial Troop Militia.

The young generation must improve and defend socialism

January 8, 1989

Distinguished guests;
Pioneers;
Students;
Young workers;
Fellow citizens:

I don't know which anniversary or which day or which period was the hardest, whether it was thirty years ago when the revolution triumphed or now, when we're commemorating the thirtieth anniversary.

These days have been full of activities. One evening I learned that you Pioneers had organized a Victory Motorcade and wanted me to take part in the rally. I told you I had

---

This speech was given at a rally commemorating the thirtieth anniversary of Castro's arrival in Havana together with the bulk of the victorious Rebel Army troops. The rally was held in Ciudad Libertad (Liberty City), formerly Camp Columbia, the main army base under the Batista regime, and now a school. The audience was made up primarily of students and Pioneers, members of Cuba's children's organization.

many activities but that there was no way I could refuse to join you, so I asked you to invite Pioneers, students, young workers, some representatives of the students from sister nations studying on the Isle of Youth, [*Applause and shouts of "Fidel! Fidel!"*] and to invite the people.

The memory of that day when we arrived in the capital will never be erased. We had crossed the island practically from one tip to the other and a sea of people welcomed our motorcade everywhere. Thirty years have gone by since then.

Like today, there was a big crowd gathered here, perhaps bigger than this one since there was more space then. This was then a big military camp and the fate of the country was decided here, and that day it was full of people. It wasn't a school, as it is today. There was great symbolism in the fact that the people gathered in precisely this military camp. It meant that the history of coups d'état, the history of military dictatorships had disappeared for good in our homeland. [*Applause*] It meant that repression and crime had disappeared for good in our country. From that time on, defending the people and the country would no longer simply be the task of the armed forces but of the entire people.

I cannot forget that crowd gathered here more or less at this same time of day. I don't even remember well all the details, but I do know that the rally ended late, very late. I think it was after midnight.

Those who were in their twenties are now in their fifties; those who were in their thirties are now in their sixties; and those who were over forty are now over seventy or eighty. Some of those people are, inevitably, no longer among us; many, however, surely have a vivid memory of that day. It's possible that today the immense majority of those gathered here—not to say nearly all of you, bearing in mind the high proportion of young people present here—had not been born on that January 8.

I don't know whether it will be easy for you to feel the emotions experienced then by our compatriots, because you didn't live through the days of horror, humiliation, and suffering they lived through.

In our nation there were many things to do. The problems we had then are not those of today; we had a whole world to change, we had a revolution to make.

I remember that our main concern that night was the question of unity among the revolutionary forces, preventing splits and clashes from breaking out among those who had fought against the dictatorship, avoiding conflicts and divisions among our people. For as Martí had believed, it was precisely conflicts and divisions that had made victory impossible in the Ten Years War. And throughout our history divisions had made it very difficult for independence to fully triumph in our nation.

At the time, that was one of the most important problems and questions. I remember that a dramatic appeal was made for unity of all the revolutionary fighters. That appeal worked, it was successful, it bore fruit.

I also remember something I said that evening of January 8, that we would always have the necessary patience once revolutionary power was in our hands, and that if the day ever came when our patience ran out we would always seek more patience, all the patience required to assume the responsibilities and enormous power that a triumphant revolution bestows on its leaders.

I believe we've been faithful to those two ideas. We have been tireless fighters for the unity of our people throughout these thirty years and we've been tireless defenders of the principle of patiently and generously exercising the power the revolution bestowed at that time on our men, our revolutionary movement and, later on, the party and the state. Those two principles proclaimed that evening have remained inviolable.

We also expressed the idea that however difficult the road might have seemed up to that moment, we were certain it would be a lot easier than the road ahead of us. We were always aware of that reality, we harbored no illusions. We had also been saying all along that this time the hour of the revolution had indeed come, that the revolution would become an inexorable reality.

I believe that the changes that took place in our country have been extraordinary; the tasks we tackled then are not those of today. At that time we had a triumphant revolution within a capitalist country, within an imperialist neocolony. That entire social system had to be demolished. The ownership of our industries, our public services, our land, our mineral resources, banking, trade, practically everything, was in the private hands of a minority of exploiters. And a significant portion of all that wealth and those industries was in the hands of foreign corporations. Our people worked for those capitalists, to enrich that class more and more, to enrich those foreign corporations more and more. One could not even conceive of our society without that system.

Nowadays it seems quite natural for you to find that wherever you go, everything is the property of the entire people, whether it's a movie theater, a warehouse, a factory, or an important plant, whether large or small. Public services, bus transportation, railroad transportation, sea transportation, schools, hospitals, research centers, the mass media—television, radio, newspapers, printshops—all that is now the people's property. If you come to a mine, if you come to big sugarcane or rice plantations or big centers producing citrus fruit or food for the population, or producing milk, meat— all that is the property of the entire people.

There still exist small properties of farmers who back then had to pay rent; an important portion of what they produced had to be turned over in payment to the big landowners. Those small farmers were exempted from all forms of rent and given the ownership of their land. This is, in the main, the only private ownership of the means of production now existing in our country.

Homes were not the property of the people. Most housing belonged to the landlords, individuals who owned 50, 100, 500, even a few thousand apartments. And the people had to pay 20, 30 percent of the family income for rent.

Nowadays every family knows that the home where they live belongs to them, that no one is going to evict them from it. The only people who are not home owners are those who live in places linked to or controlled by a factory, and they are a small minority.

Back then we could not even have dreamed of anything like that. A family could go on for thirty, forty, fifty years paying 20, 25, or 30 percent of its income in rent for a home, and never become its owner.

Back then there were the quite common phenomena of unemployment and underemployment. I remember that evening on January 8 some people shouted: "We need jobs, we need jobs!" because the problem of unemployment was a permanent scourge on that society. One could likewise have shouted, we need hospitals, we need polyclinics, we need schools, we need to give all the country's children an opportunity to study in elementary schools, junior high schools, or senior high schools. Only a tiny percentage of children could go to school—not even 50 percent of them attended elementary schools, and an insignificant proportion, less than 10 percent, attended secondary schools.

Not only could one have shouted, we need factories, we need construction, we need agricultural development; but equally, we need hospitals, we need universities, we need research centers. Because those were pressing demands in our country.

Actually, our people did not have much political awareness then, that has to be admitted. Our people did not then have the level of political awareness they later acquired. They were a militant people, an enthusiastic people, a warmhearted people, a rebellious people, a people who hated crime, injustice, abuse, corruption, and embezzlement, all the vices that characterized politics in capitalist times. They were, above all, a people who hated oppression, and that was why there was an extraordinary joy prevailing in those times.

But we could not say that it had yet become a socialist people or a Marxist-Leninist people. Back then a large part of the population was still confused. There had been dozens of years of antisocialist and anticommunist propaganda stemming from the capitalist West, mainly from the United States.

Anticommunism and antisocialism were the main banners; they were weapons to try to preserve the capitalist system intact and to try to keep the people divided. It was necessary to wage a great battle against those reactionary ideas, against that lack of awareness, because the people wanted changes but they did not have a clear idea of what changes were needed. The people were against injustice, against hunger, against unemployment, against the intolerable poverty afflicting most of the people. But they did not yet fully understand that those problems stemmed from the capitalist system, from private ownership of the means of production, from a system that by nature is exploitative, from a system that by nature is wholly unconcerned about the people's problems and only cares about the profits of the insatiable capitalist class.

If you asked people whether they wanted agrarian reform, they said yes. If you asked people whether they wanted a cut in rent, they were in agreement. If you asked about urban reform, they were in agreement; about freeing the peasants from middlemen, from all forms of exploitation, they were in agreement. If you asked them whether the public services, that is, telephones, electricity, transportation, or the large factories and the big banks, ought to be the property of the entire people, they were in agreement.

But if you asked some citizens whether they agreed with socialism, they said no, not with socialism, no. They didn't know what socialism was, they didn't know what communism was. Our people were so saturated with that propaganda that a large part of the population was not in agreement with socialism or communism, without even knowing what socialism or communism were.

That's why during the first stage of the revolution it was necessary to implement the Moncada Program[1]—it was generally accepted that it was, so to speak, the forerunner of socialism but it was not quite socialist. It did not yet speak of building socialism in our country.

How did our people become a socialist people? It was the revolutionary laws more than words, preaching, or reasoning that made our people socialist. When rents were cut, which profoundly affected the interests of those landlords, the entire people supported the measure. When the agrarian reform was carried out the entire people supported the decision. The interests of the workers were taken care of. Social justice was implemented with a strong hand from one end of the country to the other. For the first time in our country's history, the state and the government ceased being on the side of the rich and put themselves on the side of the poor. When the vast majority of our population saw that the government resolutely attacked the interests of the rich and the bourgeoisie to support the people, little by little all those lies and that whole antisocialist and anticommunist campaign came tumbling down like a house of cards. In this way a new political thinking, a true political awareness was created among our people.

Never before had such fundamental changes taken place in the social life of our country. Never before had such fundamental changes taken place with regard to the means of production. Never before had such a profound change taken place in the people's consciousness.

When slavery was abolished—and the abolition of slavery last century was the product of the heroic struggle waged by our *mambí* independence fighters in the war of 1868—in theory the slaves were freed but in actual practice they went on working for the landowners, the plantation owners, and the capitalists in exchange for a wage of next to nothing. Property did not go to the slaves, property did not go to the people.

Even when the independence of Cuba was formally proclaimed at the beginning of the century and an allegedly Cuban government was installed, with the constitution that carried an amendment, the so-called Platt Amendment, entitling the United States to intervene in our country, this did not change anything. The ownership of the land and industry continued to be in the hands of those who owned them: the plantation owners, the capitalists, the landowners, and a growing number of foreign corporations. There was absolutely no change.

With the revolutionary triumph of January 1959, for the first time in the history of our nation, property was transferred from the hands of the exploiters into the hands of the people; for the first time a true social revolution took place; for the first time a profound change took place in our people's political philosophy and consciousness. As could be expected, this unleashed the hatred and antagonism of the U.S. imperialists. They could not conceive of anything like it; they could not conceive of a socialist revolution in our country. They viewed our country as their property and our people as a herd of sheep.

Following those deep-going changes in our country's social reality, property ownership, and consciousness, a merciless imperialist blockade was launched against our country, which has already lasted as long as our revolution.

There are many tasks that the present generation no longer has to tackle. The present generation must wage ideological battles, but of another type, not to create a socialist consciousness but to defend that socialist consciousness. They don't have to wage a battle to change property ownership but to defend the system of socialist ownership. They must develop and improve that system, they must develop and improve that consciousness.

The current generation does not have to wage a battle against illiteracy because for a long time now, since 1961, illiteracy has been practically eradicated here. I don't mean to say it was eradicated in one day, but that year it began to be eliminated completely.

The younger generation does not have to build schools all over the mountains, countryside, and cities of our country. The younger generation does not have to tackle the problem of finding teachers for the schools. The younger generation does not have to tackle those tasks because all those tasks were carried out by the revolution long ago.

The younger generation, the current generation, does not have to tackle the task of bringing health care to all the people, building hospitals in the countryside and the cities. The younger generation does not have to face countless diseases that no longer exist here and it does not have to face a high infant mortality rate. It does not have to face the task of creating a hospital system throughout the country, just as in the field of education it does not have to face the task of building thousands upon thousands of new schools.

The younger generation does not have to tackle the desperate task of training tens of thousands of teachers or tens of thousands of doctors, because our country has advanced a considerable distance along that road. Today our country even has thousands upon thousands of teachers in reserve and each year our country is graduating more doctors than were left here after the revolution triumphed.

The younger generation does not have to tackle the phenomenon of unemployment.

The younger generation does not have to face the task of making the deep-going changes that were necessary in the countryside, of implementing a radical transformation. It does not have to enact new agrarian laws. It does not have to build state farms. It does not have to set up cooperatives. It does not have to free the peasants from paying rent.

The younger generation does not have to implement an urban reform.

The younger generation does not have to nationalize the mines, because they are all nationalized now. It does not have to nationalize public services, transportation—all that is done. It does not have to nationalize the factories. It does not have to nationalize education. It does not have to nationalize health services. All that is done.

We might even say that the younger generation does not have to tackle the job of building tens of thousands of kilometers of roads and highways. It does not have to face the task of building the large number of dams and minidams existing now in our country or irrigation systems or canal systems. The younger generation will not have to engage in the task of developing the country's infrastructure, the ports, railroads, and other needs of the country.

Many things done here over the past thirty years signify that as the fourth decade of the revolution begins, the tasks of this generation will be quite different—which does not mean they will be any less far-reaching or less important.

The construction of socialism in our country has gone a long way. Neither does this younger generation have to face the task of creating, organizing, and developing a party, the youth organizations, or the powerful mass organizations of the revolution. Such institutions already exist.

The current generation does not have to face the task of organizing a powerful army for the defense of the country or of organizing the defense mechanisms involving the entire people. All that has already been created.

The current generation does not have to organize the Ministry of the Interior and the instruments with which to fight against enemy activities or in defense of internal order. Those institutions have already been created.

Many things have been created but, I repeat, the responsibilities and tasks of the current generation are quite big.

First, it has to carry forward the revolution. The revolution is not the task of one day or one year or ten years or thirty years. The revolution is something that extends indefinitely over time.

The revolution has brought forth new ideas, a new ideology. The task of the current generation is developing those ideas, developing that ideology, and resolutely defending that ideology. [*Applause*]

The current generation has the task of consolidating the revolution, improving the revolution, and defending the revolution. The current generation has the task of strengthening our nation's defense mechanisms in order to defend the country's integrity and independence. The younger generation must improve and develop socialism and defend socialism. Some may have thought that stage was already over. Our opinion and our deepest conviction, however, is that this stage is now before us more than ever before.

During these thirty years the revolution defended itself against imperialist threats, imperialist aggressions, imperialist plans, imperialist subversion, imperialist crimes. It defended itself against the counterrevolutionary bands, mercenary invasions, plans to sabotage our economy, attempts to assassinate revolutionary leaders, repeated threats of direct aggression, and an economic blockade that has already lasted thirty years. But imperialism has not disappeared, imperialism is right there. Capitalist ideology has not disappeared and neither has capitalism. Capitalism and capitalist ideology are right there. Imperialism's threats have not disappeared, they are right there.

It would be an illusion to think that the whole difficult period for the revolution and for the nation is over. That would be an illusion that the current generation and the coming generations can never harbor. Imperialism has not renounced the idea of liquidating socialism in Cuba, of liquidating revolutionary ideology in Cuba; imperialism has not renounced the idea of liquidating our revolution. Imperialism might change its tactics, its weapons, but U.S. imperialism is too arrogant, too high-handed, too haughty to renounce the idea of overturning the Cuban revolution, to renounce the idea of liquidating socialism in Cuba.

Even more we can say that imperialism and capitalism worldwide are too arrogant, too high-handed, too haughty to renounce the idea of liquidating socialism on a world scale.

Imperialism has not renounced the idea of liquidating socialism in the world, of eradicating the socialist process in the world. It tried to do so more than once by force of arms, as happened during the intervention in the Soviet Union in the early years of the revolution, in the fascist aggression on the Soviet Union during World War II, in the encirclement with military and atomic bases of the Soviet Union and the socialist camp during many years as a threat to liquidate socialism through war. Of course, if historical circumstances have prevented imperialism from liquidating socialism by war, imperialism has not renounced the idea of liquidating socialism by means of subversion, corrosion, and, if possible, destruction of the socialist system from within. Perhaps to the degree that the danger of a world war becomes more distant, the efforts of capitalism and imperialism to defeat socialism in the field of ideology grow more persistent.

I believe that in this field, although the current generation does not have to plant the seed of socialism and Marxism-Leninism in the political and revolutionary thinking of our people, the current generation is faced with the pressing task of undertaking a difficult battle—although increasingly more subtle and complex—in defense of the ideas of socialism and in the ideological field.

The imperialists openly proclaim that when this revolutionary generation leaves the scene, when the generation of the people who made the war and carried out the revolution is no longer present, their task will be easier. The imperialists don't conceal their hope that it will be easier to deal with the new generations. They say, think, and calculate that since the new generations did not experience capitalism, since they did not suffer or know about the terrible experiences of the past, the new generations will have less means of comparing past and present; that the new generations will have less commitment to the revolution and be easier to distort and confuse; that it will be easier to beguile them with their models of consumer societies, fighting the ideological battles with the new generations; that in short it will be easier to defeat the revolutionary spirit of the new generations. This is openly proclaimed by the theoreticians of capitalism and imperialism. This is openly proclaimed by the political research centers of imperialism. Those are their illusions.

On the other hand, the campaign against our country has now been stepped up. It's as if now the Cuban revolution, the firmness of the Cuban revolution, the intransigence of the Cuban revolution—which is firm, determined, courageous, brave, and resolute—gives imperialism and capitalism sleepless nights. Therefore, a large part of their media organs and propaganda outlets are directed toward attacking us, toward depriving the Cuban revolution of prestige, toward trying to confuse our people.

As we said recently, there is at present a sort of imperialist euphoria, a capitalist euphoria, in view of the reforms and self-criticism taking place in various socialist countries.

This mood within world reaction is no secret to us; we are well aware of this, their euphoria that attempts to depict capitalist mechanisms as the only efficient ones for solving problems, for achieving productivity and development. We are now observing these ideas and these illusions on the part of imperialism.

They are irritated by Cuba's firm stand, by the total confidence of our country, our party, and our revolution in socialism, by our profound and intransigent Marxist-Leninist and revolutionary convictions. This intransigence is not new, it is as old as the history of our country. It is as old as the heroic Baraguá Protest, which was 100 years old in 1978. Firmness and intransigence in our people's revolutionary thinking is more than 100 years old, so the attitude of our party and our people should not surprise the imperialists. [*Applause*]

If this is the case, the current generation will understand the enormous task on its shoulders. In a way, it is an even greater task than the one we had, for at the time of the victory of the revolution socialism was prospering and united, without difficulties and with growing prestige.

What does this generation have to carry forward the work of the revolution? What does it have that we did not? In the early years we did not have teachers and now there are more than 270,000 teachers and professors. In the early years a second grade education was the norm and now it is ninth grade. In the early years there were virtually no planners, engineers of different kinds, economists, or accountants; now we have hundreds of thousands of university graduates. In the early years there were 3,000 doctors and now we have more than 30,000. The human resources available to this generation did not exist in the early years of the revolution; this generation has many thousands of scientists and technicians.

In many aspects that shape the future, our country occupies an outstanding position. In advanced technologies, which will shape Cuba's future development, we have the Center for Genetic Engineering and Biotechnology as well as the National Scientific Research Center. We recently created a center for robotic studies and one for transplants and nerve regeneration. For the last few years we have been making great gains in research on computer science. Both in electronics and in the computer and nuclear industries—for exclusively peaceful purposes, of course—there are many thousands of scientists and technicians.

We can say that in areas of scientific and technical development our country has created favorable conditions and has reached noteworthy levels.

I haven't mentioned medicine. I believe that in these years conditions have been created for our country to become a real medical power. [*Applause*]

In the field of education, conditions have been created for our country to become a real educational power as well. The latest addition in this field are the senior high schools of exact sciences, where many thousands of young people receive an education under extremely favorable conditions. [*Applause*]

Computer studies have been set up not only at institutions of higher learning, but in the teacher training schools, and very soon in all the secondary schools in the country. [*Applause*] The Union of Young Communists came up with the idea of the computer clubs, to teach those young people who did not get such studies when they were in high school or the university.

In the scientific field we have more than 100 institutions; in other fields such as inventions and the work of the Technological Youth Brigades, we have made considerable progress. All this creates conditions for the current generation to consolidate, improve, and develop socialism. [*Applause*]

We face a tremendous historic challenge. Who will win?

Who will prevail? The selfish, chaotic, and inhumane capitalist system? [*Shouts of "No!"*] Or the more rational and humane socialist system? [*Shouts and prolonged applause*] This is the challenge that now faces not just Cuban youth and the Cuban people, but the youth and peoples of all the socialist countries.

Of course this is a task for all of us and especially the new generation, which will have to make a special effort to better itself.

We must have a clear understanding of what we face and the battle in which we are involved to improve socialism in our country. And perhaps the greatest challenge is that this is a battle to improve socialism without resorting to the mechanisms and style of capitalism, without playing at capitalism. [*Applause*] That's what we are trying to do in the process of rectification.

A few days ago I said that we're starting to see some results of this process. We have seen some examples; to mention one, the contingents of construction workers. I believe that we have with us a group of the young people working in the Havana contingents. [*Applause*] In these days we have witnessed great feats: we have seen what the Blas Roca Contingent did, what the Sixth Congress Contingent did, what the contingents that built ExpoCuba did. [*Applause*] We have seen what the minibrigades did there, we have seen what the contingents in different provinces are doing. And we have seen the principles these groups of workers are applying, which have nothing in common with capitalist methods of motivation nor capitalist methods of organization. [*Applause*] I am sure there are no groups of workers like that anywhere else.

This shows what man can do; what man can do when there is faith in man, trust in man, when you don't start from the premise that man is like a little animal who only moves when you dangle a carrot in front of him or whip him with a stick. [*Applause*] The minibrigades, contingent workers, and hundreds of groups of workers in our country that are now making great efforts, and we could say thousands of groups of workers, don't act or do what they do because of a carrot or a stick. [*Applause*]

What carrot or what stick was used on the Sixth Congress Contingent, which in barely a year has just finished building—and done an excellent job—a big hospital in the capital? [*Applause*] What carrot or what stick motivated the minibrigade and contingent members who in barely a year—because the bulk of the work was done in a year—have built the tremendous ExpoCuba project? [*Applause*] What carrot or what stick was used on the citizens who put in 400,000 hours of voluntary work in building the Miguel Enríquez Hospital? [*Applause*] What carrot or stick led thousands of senior high school and technological students to put in millions of hours of voluntary work on social projects? [*Applause*]

What carrot or stick led secondary school students in the citrus project in Jagüey to harvest more than 400,000 tons of citrus fruit? [*Applause*] What carrot or stick motivated the students on the Isle of Youth, who harvested about 200,000 tons of citrus fruit? What carrot or stick motivates the tens of thousands of university students who undertake anything asked of them? [*Applause and shouts of "For sure, Fidel, give the Yankees hell!"*] What carrot or stick motivates the hundreds of thousands of students now in the School Goes to the Countryside program? [*Applause and revolutionary slogans*] What carrot or stick motivates hundreds of thousands of students who work three hours a day in the schools in the countryside? [*Applause and shouts of "For sure, Fidel, give the Yankees hell!"*]

But in relation to other fields, we could also ask: What carrot or what stick motivated the fighters of the Rebel Army who for two years confronted and defeated the army of the tyranny? [*Applause and shouts of "For sure, Fidel, give the Yankees hell!"*] What carrot or stick motivated many thousands of teachers, doctors, or workers who have rendered internationalist service? [*Applause*] What carrot or stick motivated the 50,000 Cuban fighters in Angola who made possible the victory? [*Exclamations and prolonged applause*]

A final question for the list, which could go on forever: What carrot or what stick motivated the 300,000 Cubans who honorably fulfilled their internationalist missions in Angola over the last thirteen years? [*Exclamations and prolonged applause*]

So are we or are we not correct in trusting in people, in their consciousness and spirit of solidarity? Are we or are we not right in feeling people can really do what they set out to do; that people can live in a society that is more humane, more just, more generous, and more based on solidarity than is capitalism, where the law of the jungle prevails? Could a society educated in the selfish ideas of capitalism carry out a single one of these things we've mentioned? That's why our confidence in the future of the revolution is so unshakable.

So in the light of all these experiences and factors, I was telling you that it will be your task to improve and develop the concept of socialism and the socialist system.

I'm always reading international news dispatches and often the international capitalist news agencies depict us as naive or idealistic. I don't deny that at a certain time we have been idealistic—all of us have been, in the best sense of the term. At one point we said we had made idealistic errors; but then we fell into market mania. Correcting one error, we fell into the other.

They are trying to spread confusion, saying that we are departing from the socialist formula. I want to say here categorically that we are not departing from the socialist formula, which was defined long ago, which says that each person should contribute according to his ability and receive according to his work. That means distribution is based on the quantity and quality of work that a citizen contributes to society.

In this stage of the revolution we cannot depart from that formula and the problem is how that formula should be interpreted. It's not always possible to apply the principle of giving each according to the quality and quantity of work. When we send a worker's child to school we don't consider how much his father works or how much he contributes, because the state seeks to give all children the best possible education. If a child gets sick we don't go around asking about the quality or quantity of work contributed by the mother or father; we simply view him as a child to which society and socialism have a sacred duty to care for and cure regardless of cost. If he needs cardiovascular surgery, which for a child can cost thousands of pesos, nobody hesitates in going through with it. When a kidney transplant is needed, nobody hesitates. If a heart transplant were needed, no one would hesitate. The person is not asked where he works and how much he does or doesn't contribute. A heart transplant in the United States costs 100,000 pesos. There have been dozens of heart transplants here and I would like to know if anyone has been charged a cent or if anyone has been asked about his contribution to society.

It is logical for wages to be based on the quality and quantity of work, it's a logical socialist formula. But in society there are many things, many services, many tasks, and many obligations that depart from this formula.

In the construction of socialism and without deviating from the socialist formula of giving to each according to his ability and according to his work, there are many forms and certain principles of socialism that are applied in different ways, and it can't be otherwise. There are many benefits under socialism that may resemble the formulas of communism. How much do we charge a child who has a school scholarship or who's at the university, in a technological institute, or at a school of exact sciences? How much do we charge and what child is asked about his parents' contribution? [*Applause*] We analyze the talent and merits of the child, youth, or adolescent, his grades and overall academic record; that's what the exams are for and they are given the opportunity. That yardstick, the simplistic formula of giving to each according to his ability and the quantity of his work, cannot always be used.

Of course we will not depart from the socialist formula and we understand the importance of the socialist formula of payment. We realize there are laws and principles from which we cannot depart.

We understand the importance of payment according to this norm and even the need for material incentives, we understand it. But by no means does that mean we will worship material incentives or view them as the fundamental factor.

Departing from the socialist formula of payment at this stage in the historical process of our revolution could have negative consequences, but—I'll say it over and over again— I think there are other factors that are more important than material incentives. [*Applause*]

Capitalist society is based on material incentives and it does not pay any attention to moral factors. Building socialism cannot follow the capitalist formula of giving the main weight to material incentives. I already gave many examples of accomplishments where material incentives play no role. We cannot speak of building socialism if we don't give all due weight to the moral factor and consciousness.

On January 4 I was really impressed when giving out diplomas to some workers at ExpoCuba who had made a tremendous effort. I remember one compañero who was always working; whenever I went day or night I would always find him there. He contributed 3,500 hours of voluntary work. I did some figuring and found it was the equivalent of almost two years of work, in voluntary hours after his eight-hour day. [*Applause*] What motivates that man, what amount of money? No money can buy that.

I see the men of the Blas Roca and other contingents. I see what they do and I can assure you that nobody would do what they do for money because they could earn enough to live on by doing only half of what they do. However, we have to keep fighting with them—not to make them work but so they won't work so hard, because honor is tremendously powerful, infinitely strong. If they had promised to do something and it rained and they were unable to work one day, they want to stay until 2:00 or 3:00 a.m. and we have to tell them not to go beyond 10:00 p.m. We have to hold them back and I know that's not a matter of money. They are paid, the socialist formula is applied. Voluntary work has even been banned on weekdays so they won't put in more hours. We told them, "No more voluntary work, except on Sunday." We allow it on Sunday and you can see their conduct; they respond to other motivations and considerations.

Attention to people is very important. People will do things as a result of a kind gesture that they would not do for money. Because of a kind gesture people will even lay down their lives, because of a kind gesture by the homeland men die in combat, men die in combat for ideas, for love of country, for love of ideas. [*Applause*]

The people who have run risks, the hundreds of thousands of Cubans who have risked their lives on internationalist missions, what amount of money could have paid for that? Nobody gives his life for money, since when you die there is no need for money. Nobody gives his life for a million or ten million pesos. But people are capable of giving their lives en masse for ideas.

When we mobilize, train, and arm millions of citizens of

this country to confront an invasion, we know millions are ready to die. What can we pay them with? How much will we give each of the men and women of our armed forces, the Territorial Troop Militia, and the Production and Defense Brigades, for defending the homeland? They are defending an idea, the sacred value of the homeland! [*Applause*] What amount of money will we give the combatants going on internationalist missions, the hundreds of thousands who went and risked their lives for an idea, for a principle, for solidarity, for internationalism, for honor?

What men do for honor and moral principles—when I say men, I mean men and women—what human beings do for moral principles and honor they won't do for all the money in the world. And I think it is an insult to the revolutionary ideal, to revolutionary ideas, to claim that man is only motivated by material interests.

I want to make this clear so we won't be misunderstood. We have our feet on the ground, very firmly on the ground! That is why we consider all these examples, and I've enumerated some unique examples, which are part of the education of our young people.

There cannot be socialism or a communist society without education, without having certain ideas become indispensable ethical principles for every citizen and every human being.

It is in this light that the younger generation, this generation, must work, must create, and must improve our system.

We have made important progress but more is needed now. Possibly this generation won't be building communism or living in a communist society, but it will make big progress and other generations will do likewise. It is an advance that cannot be stopped and in which generations come one after the other, like in the Victory Motorcade where there were replacements all along the way.

As I said before, there are many fields in which we have

made progress, in which the country won't have to make them the central emphasis in the future. Health care won't have to become the central emphasis, although we will have to continue improving what has been done; there are now more than 25,000 medical students. The doctors we'll need in 1995 are already in medical school and the others who will study medicine are in senior high school. We must continue these programs, logically enough, and we will have 65,000 or 70,000 doctors by the year 2000; we already know what they will do.

We must continue the family doctor program. We must continue to build polyclinics in some places, the necessary family doctor home-offices, other medical facilities, some hospitals. But it won't have to become the central emphasis in the future.

Education won't have to become the central emphasis of our investments, although we must continue to improve our programs, our school system, make it better and better, more and more scientific. Everything we're doing with the senior high schools of exact sciences or what we're doing with computers throughout secondary and university education are quality advances in that area.

We'll have to continue to build more schools, not because we're short of schools but rather to have newer, better schools, with all the adequate material conditions, not having too many pupils in one classroom, with better ventilation, better lighting, schools open to semiboarding students. We will continue to build schools, but this is one task where we have made considerable advances.

We'll continue to build dams, although generally speaking, we've already built the biggest ones, or at least an important number of them. We simply have to keep the same pace and the moment will come when even the last dam will have been built in this country and when even the last canal that could be built will have been built. There might even emerge complex engineering works built in lowlands or shallow waters. It's all a question of keeping up the pace so that we don't drop it and forget about everything. But we've made considerable advances in all that. We'll have to continue to build more roads and highways, but the bulk of the work is already done, the bulk is done!

We'll have to continue to build the National Highway starting from Santiago de Cuba and ending up on the other end in Pinar del Río. We'll have to continue to build the two-way railroad tracks leading west. These are development tasks that must be done. When we can, we must build a second track for the Central Railroad. I think it was a mistake not to have done so when it was rebuilt. We've advanced in many of these things.

We must continue to advance in the scientific research centers, making them more and more selective, knowing very well the purpose of each one of them, what usefulness it has, like with all the new scientific centers we're building. In addition, the principle of dedication to work has emerged in these centers, the principle of dedication to work! Because scientists in these new centers work long beyond their established workday.

We must continue to industrialize the country. That is the fundamental task for the next thirty years and the next sixty years. What we have to do is make the investments that reap better fruit, yield better results, solve more problems, sticking to well-chosen priorities. The current generation must go on working in this without letup and look for the means, look for the resources with which to industrialize the country.

We must continue to develop services of every kind. This is a field where the revolution has much work to do, where we have a lot to improve. I don't mean health or education services, I mean other types of services that we must find a solution for.

There is one task of great importance and that is housing construction. We'll have to place the main emphasis of social development on that in the coming years.

In other words, there are many tasks to be carried out and continued, plus other new tasks.

The steel and iron and machine industry must be developed, automatization must be mastered, we must make progress in building robots, computerized lathes, automatization, because they not only increase productivity but also improve the quality of what's produced. These are fields that the new generation must develop as much as possible and it has great potential to do so.

We must develop genetic engineering and biotechnology and we have the right conditions to do so. Electronics and computers must be given a big boost in coming years. The biological sciences must be given all the necessary attention. In agriculture, we must continue to increasingly apply science and technology and give it a boost.

We must develop programs guaranteeing a solid food supply on the basis of our climate and natural resources. Recently we've made important progress in the utilization of sugarcane as animal feed. Every hectare of Cuban land planted in cane can yield 50 percent more; with irrigation, fertilizers, and plot drainage it could double the yield and a good portion of that increase could be used to produce more meat and milk, to produce calories and proteins for cattle feed, thus creating a solid food supply with our own resources.

We must continue to expand rice programs to raise production by 50 percent. Root vegetables, green vegetables, citrus and other fruit production must be increased to feed the population. We have a big task ahead of us but there are already thousands upon thousands of university-level technicians and professionals in agriculture. That can already be seen; all the conditions are present for that.

In the field of socioeconomic development, there's a fundamental task ahead for the current generation. It must improve socialism and develop it, take it as far as possible and do so with mass methods, socialist methods, revolutionary methods. We should not let ourselves be carried away by the illusion that it can be done with capitalist methods, with vulgar capitalist methods, which are totally alien to what I was explaining here. And it can't be done by exacerbating and deifying material incentives in order to try to build socialism, because we would fail. And this is nothing new, I'm not saying it for the first time. Many years ago, one of the most intelligent and brightest revolutionaries, Che Guevara, explained this with great emphasis. [*Applause*] Many of the warnings given by Che on this matter later became reality.

The task of improving socialism is the strategic task of the current generation, the ideological struggle, defending socialism, defending ourselves from the imperialist ideological offensive. And it must be done not just with enthusiasm, not just with conviction and morale but also with thinking, study, and a deep-going analysis of our problems. Both things are essential: conviction, feelings, and enthusiasm— but you have to analyze in depth, you have to study. And, of course, I think that the teaching of revolutionary doctrine, of Marxism-Leninism, and the giving of political instruction have to be done less dogmatically and more dialectically, which doesn't mean more liberal and more opportunistic. We must interpret ideas dialectically rather than interpreting them liberally or opportunistically.

I believe we must go deeper into the history of our country. We have fabulous historical roots, incomparable examples in our history. We must get to know more about the history of Cuba, not just in school but through propaganda and books. There are times when we go crazy publishing any old book and we don't publish a good history of Cuba, even histories that have been written, biographies of historical personalities or historical accounts of past centuries—in particular the history of our society in the past, at the time when our nationality emerged, during the struggles for our independence. We must publish more books and distribute them better, books that bring us back to our cultural and historical roots, which have enormous wealth. I say there cannot be a sound political education unless there is a sound historical education; there cannot be a sound revolutionary education unless there is a sound historical education.

This generation must resist the imperialist offensive, but it must be prepared to do so in any field, for example, in the field of the country's defense. I don't want to repeat here what I said on December 5 regarding what our philosophy must be, what our concept of defense must be.

There are some people who believe or think or have said that the heroic stage is over. We should not let ourselves be carried away by such peculiar ideas, such erroneous and false views. Our heroic stage is not over and we don't know when it will be over because while some people were going around saying our heroic stage was already over, tens of thousands of men were advancing toward the south in Angola like a powerful fist, ready to liquidate the army of apartheid if it didn't fall back. So while some people were saying our heroic stage had already disappeared, never before were so many men writing such a glorious page in the history of our country. That's the reality and those things happened during 1988: on the one hand, very beautiful pages were being written while, on the other, peculiar and erratic theories were being spread.

We cannot lower our guard and we must be ready to fight. This could last for decades—I would say as long as imperialism lasts, as long as its warmongering, aggressive, threatening philosophy lasts. We see this every day. Right now Yankee ships are on their way to the Mediterranean to threaten a Third World country. And so we cannot make the mistake of neglecting our defense. We hope that the younger generation will never make that fatal mistake.

When I speak of heroism I'm not just talking about heroism in war. We need plenty of heroism in all fields; heroism in our work, we need plenty of heroism in our work. When I talked about those young men and women who got diplomas I was referring to heroes of labor. We need many heroes of labor, not just heroes willing to shed their blood—because heroes are made not just on the battlefield. Ours is a country full of men and women capable of becoming heroes. They could be heroes in construction, heroes in a factory, heroes in a scientific research center, heroes fulfilling civilian internationalist missions as teachers or doctors. The large number of doctors we now have fulfilling internationalist missions are part of our country's contingent of heroes—doctors and other professionals.

Let us hope we won't have to fight in the future! Let us hope that a climate of peace will prevail! And let us hope that in the future soldiers and fighters are replaced by doctors, teachers, scientists, and professionals! According to our country's figures, there will be 10,000 doctors ready for international cooperation by around the year 2000. Let us hope that by that time the missions we'll carry out are of that type! So when I talk about heroism, I'm not just talking about heroism on the battlefield, in the military field, but also civilian heroism, in which pages can be written as beautiful and extraordinary as those on the battlefield. In my opinion, this is a very important question, a key idea, for the current generation.

We must develop new forms and new concepts of work. We must develop the same spirit of the contingents wherever possible, not just in construction. As a matter of fact, this dedication to work began at a scientific research center. We must extend this dedication to work, not just working for the sake of working, of course, but never leaving undone what we must do because we lack manpower or time.

We must achieve a more conscious labor discipline, and a more conscious study discipline. We must leave behind all paternalistic tendencies. That's why I like so much the system of organization prevailing among the construction contingents, because in them it's the workers themselves who establish discipline.

Many laws, heaps of laws have been enacted that in some way hark back to capitalism, when workers were exploited by the capitalists. Under socialism these laws often become a hindrance, an obstacle; they have encouraged laziness and have created excessive protections that run counter to the interests of the people.

I believe there cannot be a socialist and communist consciousness until work is no longer governed by legislative norms and is no longer something imposed by society through coercion, instead of something really done in a conscious manner.

And so we will have to analyze everything concerning our own labor legislation, which was not meant to protect the good worker but rather the poor or indisciplined worker and those others who seek out twenty lawyers, twenty shysters. We must look for new forms of labor discipline, more conscious forms of labor discipline.

There is practically no absenteeism in the contingents, and no questions have to be asked because whenever one of them has had to skip work we all know he must really be sick, we all know he couldn't come to work because of something serious.

Narrow job profiles must be eradicated; they must be replaced by broader profiles. No one knows how many narrow profiles were invented here, which served only to keep workers from putting in eight hours of work. With those very narrow job profiles it was very difficult to find enough work to fill up eight hours, so people only worked for four, five, six, or seven hours. We must employ the idea of broad job profiles. It's silly to organize work so that this worker only does this and that one only does that. We have already gained experience and we're gaining more. We should not be hasty about any of these things but we must work in a sustained manner to implement these ideas. In my opinion, they are key ideas for achieving discipline, for achieving efficiency under socialism.

There is already a group of workplaces beginning to set the example.

On the other hand, we must make use of technology, master technology and apply it, for that is what labor productivity is all about. You can encourage a man to cut more cane through material incentives—and I say that cane cutting is a good example of the kind of work where applying the socialist formula cannot be abandoned—but however much you encourage a man, he might be able to cut 30 percent, 50 percent more cane. However, one machine, the KTP-1 harvester, cuts the equivalent of what forty men can do, while the KTP-2 can cut as much as sixty or seventy men can, and it's possible that later on we will have machines with which one man can cut the equivalent of what 120 can. There we have a very clear example of how productivity depends primarily on technology.

Material incentives have a limit and we must use them above all depending on the type of work involved. A computerized lathe does in two hours and with much better quality what it would take the best lathe operator fifty hours to complete. Using a computer, a draftsman or engineer can do in an hour and a half all the calculations requiring forty or sixty hours to complete without it. The secret of labor productivity and discipline lies in technology.

The productivity shown by the Blas Roca Contingent and other contingents does not depend on the speed with which a man drives a vehicle, but on his perseverance. He is prohibited from driving faster than a certain speed to protect his life, to protect the lives of others, and to take better care of the equipment. The Blas Roca Contingent's productivity depends on keeping up the pace; the vehicle comes and goes without letup. The loader is always there, the bulldozer is always there, everyone is always doing his job, no time is wasted. That's the secret of its productivity, not the truck drivers always speeding everywhere. They are prohibited from driving faster than a certain speed.

The secret of productivity lies in discipline; in technology, in rational and efficient organization, in the rational and efficient use of machinery and human resources.

That's why we must have discipline, we must develop truly scientific methods of organization and management, and we must master technology. In this way we can do much more than the capitalists—when we improve our organizational methods and when we learn to lead men and women. That's where the secret lies—using revolutionary methods.

I believe all these are tasks for the current generation—quite serious tasks. It's a historic task you'll be faced with thirty years from now. If we make evaluations every thirty years, you'll have to render an account of what you have done over the next thirty years—actually they fly by, remember that you hadn't been born when we began the last thirty years—and you'll have to meet in the future with the new generations that have not yet been born. People born on January 1, 1959—I think we have here a few dozen compañeros who were born on that day—they're now thirty years old. [Applause] Many of you, even the little Pioneers, thirty years from now will be forty, forty-one, forty-two years old; and the young people among you will be forty-some, fifty years old. There will be younger generations, like all of you are now, to whom you'll have to render an account of what you've done, and we hope that you'll be passing on to them a strong, victorious revolution, stronger and more victorious than our revolution is now. [*Applause*]

I think, to be sure, that your responsibilities are quite big and not just in our country. The tasks of this generation will not be confined only to the domestic affairs of Cuba.

We live in a hemisphere and on a continent, and that is of enormous importance. We are part of the Latin American and Caribbean peoples; together they have a population of more than 400 million, nearly double that of the United States.

This generation of Cubans has an immense and gigantic task as does this generation of Latin Americans. I see it everywhere, I see many young people, I see many brilliant people from all those countries. During these days we've seen hundreds of them, and you should see the respect and affection with which they speak about Cuba. They have made statements of all kinds supporting the revolution, explaining how much they trust it, the hopes they place in the Cuban revolution.

This is a decisive moment in the history of Latin America and the Caribbean. We note in those peoples great turmoil, great rebellion against imperialist domination such as we have never seen before. These are genuinely new times and they cannot take any more. They cannot take the consequences of the debt, unequal terms of trade, protectionism, systematic plunder, continued theft through this procedure. They can no longer take the outflow of capital, the brain drain, the conditions to which they are subjected. This is why there is turmoil in the hemisphere.

Our people face a historic task of enormous importance, that of struggling alongside the peoples of Latin America. We have the duty to be an example. We have the duty of showing solidarity. We have the duty of advancing the revolution in order to uphold and enhance the ideas of socialism and the prestige of socialism. We have the duty to cooperate and help with great enthusiasm. [*Applause*]

I would not venture to say that socialism is on the immediate agenda in Latin America, but I do venture to say that the independence of the peoples of Latin America is on the agenda. The peoples of Latin America have lost their independence, they left Spanish colonialism behind and have fallen into an even more serious form of domination, that of neocolonial and imperialist domination.

There is a historical reality: the United States was formed from a handful of British colonies on the east coast of the United States. It was later extended into the central portion of the continent, exterminating the Indians, and it reached the Pacific Coast thanks to brutal methods of extermination while also taking over more than half of Mexico. More than half of Mexico's territory was seized by the United States in an expansionist war. Then the United States intervened in Central America in various ways. It also tried to take over Cuba. I already talked about the Narciso López expedition and there were also expeditions from pirates in Central America. It took over the isthmus of Panama to build a canal and has established terrible forms of domination in all of Latin America. It was no accident that on the eve of his glorious death Martí said that everything he had done and would do was intended, before it was too late, to prevent the United States from spreading through the Antilles and falling with added weight on the lands of the Americas once Cuba was independent.

Most of the coups d'état in Latin America this century were promoted by the United States. Among the most well known was the coup against Allende that led to the Pinochet dictatorship, which has lasted more than fifteen years. In Central America it promoted coups d'état; in South America all sorts of coups. It invaded the Dominican Republic when there was a revolution there. It sent troops to Grenada, taking advantage of the mistakes and suicidal conduct of that revolutionary process. The United States has kept Cuba under constant threat. It is carrying out a genocidal war in El Salvador and a dirty war in Nicaragua.

No young person can forget these realities of our hemisphere, of our great homeland—and our great homeland is Latin America and the Caribbean. Only in that great homeland can the peoples of Latin America and the Caribbean survive! [*Applause and shouts*]

The idea of Bolívar and Martí is more relevant than ever; it is a political, economic, and historical necessity.

Great economic communities are being built in the world: the United States and Canada constitute a great economic community; Europe is a great economic community; the socialist countries of Europe form a great economic community; Japan is a great economic community; China is a great economic community and will be so more and more. Our peoples have no future without unity and integration.

These ideas are more powerful than ever. These ideas and these ties of unity and solidarity must be developed more than ever among the current generation and the peoples of Latin America. Therein lies a great and enormous task. Ties must be strengthened in every possible way. Our current struggle is very broad because we advocate unity to solve vital problems and to ensure the independence of our peoples. What's important for us is not the social system each of them should have. We're interested in all those things that unite us, and there are more things that unite us than the interests we've mentioned. We are united by the desire for peace and the respect due each of our peoples, the interest in defining what sort of world we will live in, what sort of peace we will have in the future.

Our generation was isolated, quite isolated by the imperialists, who obliged governments to break ties with Cuba, although links with the peoples of Latin America were never broken. But that period is a thing of the past and now there are broad ties in every sense with the peoples and with a growing number of governments of Latin America.

We are entering a stage in which Latin Americans are joining forces in order to survive, to achieve our independence, to develop, to have a place in the world of the future. These are tasks of great importance.

That's why I think the current generation must study not only Cuban history; it must study the history of Latin America, the geography of Latin America, the economy of Latin America, the economic and social situation in Latin America. Fortunately we all speak the same language, we have many common cultural roots. We can even communicate with those who speak Portuguese; they understand us and we understand them. The best example is in Angola, where they speak Portuguese. Nobody had to speak Portuguese to go on an internationalist mission in Angola, even as a teacher or professor. This common language and culture is a great advantage.

If we joined our culture with the cultures of all the peoples of Latin America we would create a gigantic cultural force, I would say superior to that of any other region in the world. This can be seen in the cultural meetings, the activities of Casa de las Américas, the film festivals, the theater festivals, the dance and ballet festivals, the painting biennials. In all artistic and cultural activities we can clearly see our tremendous potential and we must make it into an enormous common source of wealth.

That's why I said that we publish everything, but I wonder how many books of Latin American history we publish. What do we know about the history of Latin America and the Caribbean? What do we know about its geography, its economy, and its natural resources?

Now that we're talking about political education, political education is inconceivable without detailed information about what happens in our large and common homeland, our future destiny, which is Latin America and the Caribbean.

Some of them speak English, but English isn't so difficult and perhaps one day we will study it with greater dedication than when we were being attacked by the Yankee imperialists. Learning English isn't so difficult in order to communicate with the countries of the English-speaking Caribbean.

I think these are key questions and we can't lose time in this. I'm not talking about education in school; there should be at least a minimum of that. I'm talking about education for the entire population. Our people read, they like books. Our young people should be urged, since we all like to read scientific books or novels—and I tell you that no novel is more real, no history is more interesting than our own, no history is more interesting than the history of the peoples of Latin America. I think that's one of the tasks for this generation.

We should not be envied for having lived through certain periods of history—and we have really lived through very important periods. It is you who should be envied for the tasks you face, for the history that lies ahead, for the starting point you now have to carry forward the work of the revolution, to pursue the great tasks of our hemisphere and the world. This doesn't mean our internationalist ties will be weakened with other countries. We must continue to develop our internationalist ties with our brothers and sisters in Africa and elsewhere.

It is a great pleasure and a great privilege to have with us today participating in this ceremony representatives of eighteen African countries and other parts of the world who study on the Isle of Youth. [*Applause*] Who would have dreamed thirty years ago that on the Isle of Youth we would have more than 18,000 students from abroad? This is a source of pride and satisfaction for us. Recently I explained that we have many unique things, and I would say that the Cuban experience on the Isle of Youth is something unique in the world, the result of the internationalist feelings of our people.

[*Applause*] Just look at what it represents, how symbolic it is that Cuban youth and Pioneers should be gathering here and with them 1,000 students from other countries, representing the more than 18,000 on the Isle of Youth and the more than 24,000 now in our country.

What relationships, links, and ties these are. What a moving example of today's interrelated world. What a moving example of what the Third World means. What an inspiring example of the tasks that lie ahead. This generation must continue developing these feelings and that spirit. There is a lot we must do together with and alongside the Third World.

We must continue to develop our ties with the socialist countries, regardless of their style or model of building socialism. We have our own ideas, but we start by proclaiming our absolute respect for the right of each socialist country to try to build socialism in the manner and with the methods it sees fit. What they do does not involve us. We respect what others do just as we demand absolute respect for what we are doing. [*Applause*]

It is very important, of strategic importance, for the current generation to continue to develop those links with the socialist countries and with revolutionary forces, progressive forces, the working class, honest and progressive intellectuals, and democratic sectors in the capitalist countries. If there is a climate of peace and coexistence it would even be good to develop ties of scientific, technical, and economic cooperation with other states that are not socialist.

I believe our revolution has acquired sufficient maturity and experience in these thirty years for the new generation to be able to pursue a wise, intelligent, and fruitful policy in this field.

If I were asked, like the young compañera asked me, what could I say to you, what would I want to say, there is a lot I would like to say and it would require a lot of time.

I think you understand that the future won't fall like

manna from heaven. The goods needed to raise our people's standard of living must continue to be created and developed. They must be created in ever greater amounts and they will be the result of our work and our intelligence.

Rather than asking, we must develop the idea of giving! Distrust those who go around asking and making excessive demands. Distrust them! Because those who make unrealistic demands won't give us results. Results will have to come from those who contribute, those who give, those who create, and those who work. Only the work and intelligence of our people can fully satisfy all our needs and aspirations.

I believe it is just and legitimate to strive to fulfill these needs and aspirations. I am sure we can and will achieve this, although life is always creating new desires. I am sure, as I have said previously, that from now on we can and will transform every year into two or three years. I am sure the coming years will be more fruitful than ever.

In the same way that I say that discipline is indispensable, I feel that a demanding attitude toward everyone regarding the fulfillment of social duties must be one of the fundamental principles of the coming generations.

There is a lot I could say but I think that's enough. Perhaps I might add that our generation, called the Generation of the Centennial because it began its struggle at the time of the centennial of Martí's birth; the generation of the revolution, of January 1, 1959, believes in you, has faith in you, the generation of the thirtieth anniversary.

I know you are truly worthy sons and daughters of those who reinitiated the revolution to achieve the full independence of our homeland. And on behalf of the party and all the revolutionary fighters of my generation—older or younger—I express our absolute faith in you, our absolute confidence that you will know how to deal with the great challenges of the future, that you will struggle and prevail in the ideological struggle and for the consolidation of the revolution, the improvement of socialism, and the development of socialism. [*Prolonged applause*]

Allow me to express my complete certainty that no generation in the history of our country has ever had the privilege of seeing young people like this come up after it! [*Applause*]

Patria o muerte!

Venceremos! [*Ovation*]

Notes

Introduction

1. Fidel Castro, speech to Communist Party leaders from the city of Havana, November 29, 1987. Published in *Granma Weekly Review*, December 13, 1987; the speech was reprinted in the *Militant*, January 29, 1988.

2. Fidel Castro, speech to the deferred session of the Third Congress of the Communist Party of Cuba, December 2, 1986. Published under the title "Important Problems for the Whole of International Revolutionary Thought," *New International* no. 6, p. 296.

3. Fidel Castro, speech on the twentieth anniversary of the death of Ernesto Che Guevara, October 8 1987. Published in Ernesto Che Guevara, *Socialism and Man in Cuba* (New York: Pathfinder 2009), p. 29.

4. Ibid., p. 45.

5. Ibid., p. 39.

6. Ibid., p. 37.

As long as the empire exists we will never lower our guard
December 5, 1988

1. On the final day of his visit to Mexico, Castro visited the town of Tuxpan, where on November 25, 1956, he and eighty-one other fighters had embarked for Cuba on the yacht *Granma*.

2. During the U.S. occupation of Cuba at the beginning of the twentieth century, Washington established a naval base at Guantánamo on the southeast coast of the island. Over the protests of the Cuban people and government, the Guantánamo naval base remains there to this day.

3. In 1962, the U.S. administration of John F. Kennedy had set in

motion secret plans to invade Cuba and overthrow the revolutionary government. Cuba acquired missiles from the Soviet Union to
defend itself from the threatened U.S. aggression. In October of that
year, Washington initiated the "Cuban missile crisis" (or October
crisis) by ordering a total blockade of Cuba, threatening an immediate attack on the island, and placing U.S. forces throughout the
world on nuclear alert. The crisis abated following an agreement
between the U.S. and Soviet governments to withdraw the missiles
in exchange for a commitment by Washington not to invade Cuba.
The U.S.-Soviet accord was negotiated without the knowledge or
involvement of the Cuban government.

4. In April 1961, 1,500 Cuban-born mercenaries organized by
the U.S. government invaded Cuba at the Bay of Pigs. The invaders
immediately met a determined response by thousands of militia
members and regular troops. After seventy-two hours, the last invaders surrendered at Playa Girón (Girón Beach), which is the name
Cubans use for the battle.

5. The mountains of the Sierra Maestra in eastern Cuba were
the base from which the Rebel Army led the victorious war against
the Batista dictatorship in 1956–58. For several years in the early
1960s, the CIA organized armed counterrevolutionary bands in the
Escambray mountains in central Cuba and elsewhere. Through a
determined campaign by Cuba's regular armed forces and peasant-
based militias, these bands were eliminated by the mid-1960s.

6. Antonio Maceo was a prominent leader of Cuba's battles for
independence from Spain in the late nineteenth century.

7. Cuba's first war for independence from Spain, known as the
Ten Years War, was launched October 10, 1868, in the town of Yara,
and lasted until 1878. A second conflict, the "Little War," occurred
in 1879. The final war for independence occurred in 1895–98, leading to the end of Spanish colonial rule. It was immediately followed,
however, by a U.S. military occupation of the country.

8. Slavery was abolished in Cuba in 1886.

9. Carlos Manuel de Céspedes, Ignacio Agramonte, Máximo
Gómez, and Antonio Maceo were leaders of Cuba's 1868–78 independence war. In 1895 José Martí, considered the country's national
hero, renewed the battle for independence; Gómez and Maceo again

were among the central leaders.

10. The Platt Amendment of 1901 was imposed by the U.S. Congress on the constitution of Cuba during the U.S. military occupation of that island that began in 1898. This measure violated the country's sovereignty by granting Washington the right to intervene in Cuban affairs at any time.

11. On July 26, 1953, Castro and more than 100 fighters attacked the Moncada army garrison in Santiago de Cuba, signaling the opening of the revolutionary struggle against the Batista dictatorship. The assault failed, and many of the revolutionaries were captured, tortured, and murdered. Castro himself was arrested and imprisoned together with twenty-nine other revolutionary fighters.

12. On April 16, 1961, on the eve of the Bay of Pigs invasion, Castro delivered a speech proclaiming the socialist character of the Cuban revolution. The speech capped a year of mobilizations by Cuban workers against efforts by U.S.-owned monopolies, Cuban capitalists, and Washington to block the new Cuban government from implementing a land reform, asserting national control over the country's economic resources, and protecting the living and job conditions of working people.

13. The People's Armed Forces for the Liberation of Angola (FAPLA) are the armed forces of the Angolan government. UNITA (National Union for the Total Independence of Angola) is an organization of mercenaries backed and supplied by the U.S. and South African governments. It has been waging a terrorist war against the Angolan government and people since the mid-1970s when Angola succeeded in throwing off Portuguese colonial rule.

14. Soviet leader Mikhail Gorbachev arrived in the United States on December 7, 1987, for a summit meeting with President Ronald Reagan. During that summit the two leaders signed a treaty to reduce intermediate-range nuclear forces.

15. Adopted in 1978, Resolution 435 mandated South Africa to surrender its control of Namibia and outlined specific steps for bringing about Namibia's independence under United Nations supervision.

16. The accords were signed on December 22, 1988.

17. On December 5, 1956, three days after the *Granma* landing, the revolutionary forces were surprised by Batista's troops at

Alegría de Pío. A majority of the combatants were killed, captured, or separated from the guerrilla unit.

The Cuban people will always remain
loyal to the principles of socialism
January 1, 1989

1. In May 1958, Batista's army launched an all-out military offensive in the Sierra Maestra. The offensive was repulsed and the Rebel Army went on a counteroffensive that militarily turned the tide of the war.

2. Radio Rebelde was a station set up by the Rebel Army in the Sierra Maestra during the war, with its broadcasts eventually reaching the entire country.

3. Camp Columbia in Havana was the largest military garrison of the Batista regime and the headquarters of its general staff.

4. In 1878 Antonio Maceo issued the Baraguá Protest, famous in Cuban history, condemning the terms that ended Cuba's first independence war and vowing to continue the struggle. Mariana Grajales was a hero of the independence war and the mother of Antonio Maceo.

5. Narciso López, a former Spanish officer, organized an armed expedition that landed in Cuba in 1850 with the backing of the United States. López was taken prisoner by Spanish colonial forces and executed.

6. In 1895–96, during Cuba's final independence war against Spain, Antonio Maceo and Máximo Gómez led Cuban forces westward across the entire length of the island in the midst of fierce fighting, extending the war to the whole country.

7. Cuba's last independence war was launched in Baire on February 24, 1895. José Martí, the central organizer of Cuban forces, was killed in battle shortly afterward in the town of Dos Ríos.

8. *Mambí* is a Cuban word that refers to the nineteenth century independence fighters against Spanish colonial rule.

Thirty years of the Cuban revolution
January 4, 1989

1. This is a reference to a demand by several Latin American countries that the international coastal fishing-rights limit be ex-

tended from 12 to 200 miles. Although Cuba has developed a large oceangoing fishing fleet and would not benefit from the measure, it nevertheless joined the fight for this demand to protect the interests of the Latin American countries.

2. From late 1960 through 1961, Cuba carried out a successful literacy campaign, teaching one million Cubans to read and write. Central to this effort was the mobilization of 100,000 young people to go to the countryside, where they lived with peasants whom they were teaching.

3. A prominent German naturalist (1769–1859), Humboldt made an expedition to Cuba and Central and South America at the turn of the nineteenth century.

The young generation must improve and defend socialism
January 8, 1989

1. The Moncada Program was set forth by Fidel Castro at his 1953 trial for the attack on the Moncada garrison. Castro later reconstructed his defense speech containing that program and had it published under the title "History Will Absolve Me." It is available as an appendix in Marta Harnecker, *Fidel Castro's Political Strategy: From Moncada to Victory* (New York: Pathfinder Press, 1987).

Index

50 YEARS OF COVERT OPERATIONS IN THE US

Washington's political police and the American working class
Larry Seigle, Farrell Dobbs, Steve Clark

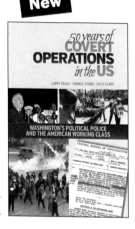

New

The 15-year political campaign of the Socialist Workers Party to expose decades of spying and disruption by the FBI and other federal cop agencies targeting working-class organizations and other opponents of government policies. Traces the origins of bipartisan efforts to expand presidential powers and build the "national security" state essential to maintaining capitalist rule. Includes "Imperialist War and the Working Class" by Farrell Dobbs. $12. Also in Spanish.

SOCIALISM ON TRIAL

New Edition

Testimony at Minneapolis Sedition Trial
James P. Cannon

The revolutionary program of the working class, as presented during the 1941 trial—on the eve of US entry into World War II—of leaders of the Minneapolis labor movement and the Socialist Workers Party on frame-up charges of "seditious conspiracy." Includes Cannon's answer to ultraleft critics of his testimony, drawing lessons from Marx and Engels to the October 1917 revolution in Russia and beyond. $16. Also in Spanish.

www.pathfinderpress.com

The Cuban Revolution and the Cuban Five

Absolved by Solidarity
16 watercolors for 16 years of unjust imprisonment of the Cuban Five
In English and Spanish, bilingual edition. $15

Voices from Prison
The Cuban Five
$7. Also in Spanish, French, Arabic, and Farsi.

"I Will Die the Way I've Lived"
15 watercolors by Antonio Guerrero
$7. Also in Spanish, French, and Farsi.

Antonio Guerrero's new book of watercolors *Absolved by Solidarity* couldn't be more timely. Along with *Voices from Prison* and Guerrero's earlier text and paintings, *"I Will Die the Way I've Lived,"* it recounts the 1998 frame up of the Cuban Five and international campaign that freed them.

Washington's frame-up "had only one purpose: punishing Cuba," Guerrero writes. With clarity and humor, these books tell the truth about that living socialist revolution and coming battles worldwide that will be fought and won by the kind of men and women only popular proletarian transformations like Cuba's can produce.

WWW.PATHFINDERPRESS.COM

WOMEN'S LIBERATION AND SOCIALISM

Cosmetics, Fashions, and the Exploitation of Women
Joseph Hansen, Evelyn Reed, Mary-Alice Waters

Sixty years ago, an article published in the socialist weekly the *Militant* sparked a lively debate on how the cosmetics and "fashion" industries play on the economic and emotional insecurities of women and youth to rake in profits. Today that exchange, contained in this book, a Marxist classic, offers an introduction to the origin of women's oppression and the struggle for liberation. $15. Also in Spanish.

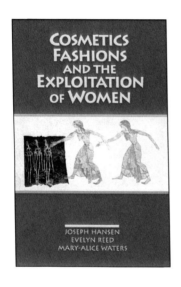

Women in Cuba: The Making of a Revolution Within the Revolution
Vilma Espín, Asela de los Santos, Yolanda Ferrer

As working people in Cuba fought to bring down a bloody tyranny in the 1950s, the unprecedented integration of women in the ranks and leadership of the struggle was not an aberration. It was intertwined with the proletarian course of the leadership of the Cuban Revolution from the start. This book is the story of that revolution and how it transformed the women and men who made it. $20. Also in Spanish.

CLASS STRUGGLE IN THE UNITED STATES

Is Socialist Revolution in the U.S. Possible?
A Necessary Debate
MARY-ALICE WATERS

"To think a socialist revolution in the US is not possible, you'd have to believe not only that the wealthy ruling families and their economic wizards have found a way to 'manage' capitalism. You'd have to close your eyes to the spreading imperialist wars and economic, financial, and social crises we are in the midst of." —MARY-ALICE WATERS

In talks given as part of a wide-ranging debate at the 2007 and 2008 Venezuela Book Fairs, Waters explains why a socialist revolution is not only possible, but why revolutionary struggles by working people are inevitable—battles forced on us by the rulers' crisis-driven assaults on our living and job conditions, on our very humanity. $7. Also in Spanish and French.

Cuba and the Coming American Revolution
JACK BARNES

The Cuban Revolution of 1959 had a worldwide political impact, including on working people and youth in the US. In the early 1960s, says Barnes, "the mass proletarian-based struggle to bring down Jim Crow segregation in the South was marching toward bloody victories as the Cuban Revolution was advancing." The deep-going social transformation Cuban toilers fought for and won set an example that socialist revolution is not only necessary—it can be made and defended by workers and farmers in the imperialist heartland as well. Foreword by Mary-Alice Waters. $10. Also in Spanish and French.

www.pathfinderpress.com

The Russian Revolution and the Fight against National Oppression

Samizdat
Voices of the Soviet Opposition
GEORGE SAUNDERS

From courageous agitation by Pussy Riot to the popular working-class uprising for national sovereignty and political rights in Ukraine, events across the former Soviet Union in the 21st century bring new life to these works clandestinely circulated hand to hand in the USSR between the 1950s and early 1970s.

Authors give firsthand accounts of the Bolshevik revolution; 1918–20 civil war; and resistance to the Stalinist political counterrevolution that reversed V.I. Lenin's proletarian internationalist course. Read about the 1953 rebellion at the Vorkuta forced-labor camp; opposition to Moscow's 1968 invasion to crush the "Prague Spring"; and struggles by Ukrainians, Tatars, and other non-Russian peoples for national rights. $25

The Revolution Betrayed
What Is the Soviet Union and Where Is It Going?
LEON TROTSKY

In 1917 workers and peasants of Russia were the motor force for one of the deepest revolutions in history. Yet within ten years a political counterrevolution by a privileged social layer whose chief spokesperson was Joseph Stalin was being consolidated. This classic study of the Soviet workers state and the degeneration of the revolution illuminates the roots of the disintegration of the Soviet bureaucracy and sharpening conflicts in and among the former republics of the USSR. $20. Also in Spanish.

The History of the Russian Revolution
LEON TROTSKY

A classic account of the social, economic, and political dynamics of the first socialist revolution as told by one of its central leaders. Trotsky describes how, under Lenin's leadership, the Bolshevik Party led the working class, peasantry, and oppressed nationalities to overturn the monarchist regime of the landlords and capitalists and bring to power a government of the workers and peasants—one that set an example for toilers the world over. Unabridged edition, 3 vols. in one. $38. Also in Russian.

Lenin's Final Fight
Speeches and Writings, 1922–23
V.I. LENIN

In 1922 and 1923, V.I. Lenin, central leader of the world's first socialist revolution, waged what was to be his last political battle. At stake was whether that revolution would remain on the proletarian course that had brought workers and peasants to power in October 1917—and laid the foundations for a truly worldwide revolutionary movement of toilers organizing to emulate the Bolsheviks' example. *Lenin's Final Fight* brings together the reports, articles, and letters through which Lenin waged this political battle. $20. Also in Spanish.

To See the Dawn
Baku, 1920—First Congress of the Peoples of the East

How can peasants and workers in the colonial world throw off imperialist exploitation? How can they overcome national and religious divisions incited by their own ruling classes and fight for their common class interests? As the example of the October Revolution echoed around the world, these questions were addressed by 2,000 delegates to the 1920 Congress of the Peoples of the East. $24

www.pathfinderpress.com

New International

A MAGAZINE OF MARXIST POLITICS AND THEORY

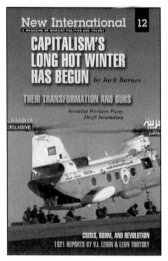

NEW INTERNATIONAL NO. 12

Capitalism's Long Hot Winter Has Begun

Jack Barnes

and *"Their Transformation and Ours,"* Resolution of the Socialist Workers Party

Today's accelerating global capitalist crisis—the opening stages of what will be decades of economic, financial, and social convulsions and class battles— accompanies a continuation of the most far-reaching shift in Washington's military policy and organization since the US buildup toward World War II. Class-struggle-minded working people must face this historic turning point for imperialism, and draw satisfaction from being "in their face" as we chart a revolutionary course to confront it. $16. Also in Spanish, French, and Arabic.

NEW INTERNATIONAL NO. 13

Our Politics Start with the World

Jack Barnes

The huge economic and cultural inequalities between imperialist and semicolonial countries, and among classes within almost every country, are produced, reproduced, and accentuated by the workings of capitalism. For vanguard workers to build parties able to lead a successful revolutionary struggle for power in our own countries, says Jack Barnes in the lead article, our activity must be guided by a strategy to close this gap.

Also in No. 13: "Farming, Science, and the Working Classes" *by Steve Clark.* $14. Also in Spanish and French.

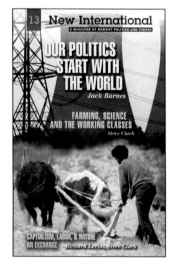

NEW INTERNATIONAL NO. 11

U.S. Imperialism
Has Lost the Cold War

Jack Barnes

Contrary to imperialist expectations in the 1990s in the wake of the collapse of regimes across Eastern Europe and the USSR claiming to be communist, the workers and farmers there have not been crushed. The toilers remain an intractable obstacle to imperialism's advance, one the exploiters will have to confront in class battles and war. $16. Also in Spanish and French.

NEW INTERNATIONAL NO. 8

Che Guevara, Cuba, and
the Road to Socialism

Articles by Ernesto Che Guevara, Carlos Rafael Rodríguez, Carlos Tablada, Mary-Alice Waters, Steve Clark, Jack Barnes

Exchanges from the opening years of the Cuban Revolution and today on the political perspectives defended by Guevara as he helped lead working people to advance the transformation of economic and social relations in Cuba. $10. Also in Spanish.

IN NEW INTERNATIONAL NO. 10

Defending Cuba, Defending Cuba's
Socialist Revolution

Mary-Alice Waters

In the 1990s, in face of the greatest economic difficulties in the history of the Cuban Revolution, workers and farmers defended their political power, independence and sovereignty, and the historic course they embarked on in 1959. Waters addresses discussions and debates in Cuba on voluntary work, income taxes on wages, farm cooperatives, and much more. In *New International no. 10*. $16. Also in Spanish and French.

THE TEAMSTER STRUGGLE

Teamster Rebellion
Teamster Power
Farrell Dobbs

Farrell Dobbs, a young
worker who became part of
the class-struggle leadership
of the Minneapolis
Teamsters in the 1930s, tells
the story of the strikes and
organizing drives that forged
the industrial union movement throughout the Midwest of the
United States. The first two of a series of four volumes written by a
central leader of these battles and the communist movement. $19
each. Also in Spanish and French.

Teamster Politics
Farrell Dobbs

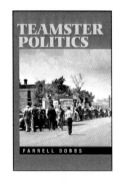

How the Minneapolis Teamsters combated FBI
frame-ups, helped the jobless organize, deployed
a Union Defense Guard to turn back fascist
thugs, fought to advance independent labor
political action, and mobilized opposition to US
imperialism's entry into World War II. $19. Also
in Spanish.

Teamster Bureaucracy
Farrell Dobbs

How the employing class, backed by union
bureaucrats, stepped up government efforts
to gag class-conscious militants; how workers
mounted a world campaign to free eighteen
union and socialist leaders framed up and
imprisoned in the infamous 1941 federal sedition
trial. $19

www.pathfinderpress.com

African freedom struggle

How Far We Slaves Have Come!
SOUTH AFRICA AND CUBA IN TODAY'S WORLD

Nelson Mandela, Fidel Castro

Speaking together in Cuba in 1991, Mandela and Castro discuss the place in the history of Africa of Cuba and Angola's victory over the invading U.S.-backed South African army, and the resulting acceleration of the fight to bring down the racist apartheid system. $10. Also in Spanish.

Thomas Sankara Speaks
THE BURKINA FASO REVOLUTION 1983–87

Colonialism and imperialist domination have left a legacy of hunger, illiteracy, and economic backwardness in Africa. In 1983 the peasants and workers of Burkina Faso established a popular revolutionary government and began to combat the causes of such devastation. Thomas Sankara, who led that struggle, explains the example set for Africa and the world. $24. Also in French.

Women's Liberation and the African Freedom Struggle
Thomas Sankara

"There is no true social revolution without the liberation of women," explains the leader of the 1983–87 revolution in Burkina Faso. $8. Also in Spanish and French.

www.pathfinderpress.com

The Cuban Revolution and

Soldier of the Cuban Revolution

FROM THE CANE FIELDS OF ORIENTE
TO GENERAL OF THE
REVOLUTIONARY ARMED FORCES

Luis Alfonso Zayas

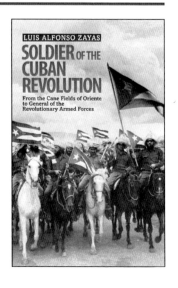

The author recounts his experiences over five decades in the revolution. From a teenage combatant in the clandestine struggle and 1956–58 war that brought down the US-backed dictatorship, to serving three times as a leader of the Cuban volunteer forces that helped Angola defeat an invasion by the army of white-supremacist South Africa, Zayas tells how he and other ordinary men and women in Cuba changed the course of history and, in the process, transformed themselves as well. $18. Also in Spanish.

Our History Is Still Being Written

THE STORY OF THREE CHINESE-CUBAN GENERALS
IN THE CUBAN REVOLUTION

In Cuba, the greatest measure against racial discrimination "was the revolution itself," says Gen. Moisés Sío Wong, "the triumph of a socialist revolution." Armando Choy, Gustavo Chui, and Sío Wong talk about the historic place of Chinese immigration to Cuba, as well as more than five decades of revolutionary action and internationalism, from Cuba to Angola and Venezuela today. Through their stories we see how millions of ordinary men and women changed the course of history, becoming different human beings in the process. $20. Also in Spanish and Chinese.

Marianas in Combat

TETÉ PUEBLA AND THE MARIANA GRAJALES WOMEN'S PLATOON
IN CUBA'S REVOLUTIONARY WAR 1956–58

Teté Puebla

Brigadier General Teté Puebla, the highest-ranking woman in Cuba's Revolutionary Armed Forces, joined the struggle to overthrow the US-backed dictatorship of Fulgencio Batista in 1956, when she was fifteen years old. This is her story—from clandestine action in the cities, to serving as an officer in the victorious Rebel Army's first all-women's unit—the Mariana Grajales Women's Platoon. For nearly fifty years, the fight to transform the social and economic status of women in Cuba has been inseparable from Cuba's socialist revolution. $14. Also in Spanish.

World Politics

Cuba and Angola
FIGHTING FOR AFRICA'S FREEDOM AND OUR OWN

The story of Cuba's nearly 16-year internationalist mission to aid the people of Angola, in the words of those who made that history, including Fidel Castro, Nelson Mandela, and Raúl Castro. With a special feature by Gabriel García Márquez. Also includes accounts by three of the Cuban Five who fought in Angola. $12. Also in Spanish.

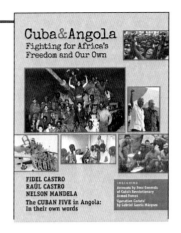

The First and Second Declarations of Havana
Nowhere are the questions of revolutionary strategy that today confront men and women on the front lines of struggles in the Americas addressed with greater truthfulness and clarity than in these two documents, adopted by million-strong assemblies of the Cuban people in 1960 and 1962. These uncompromising indictments of imperialist plunder and "the exploitation of man by man" continue to stand as manifestos of revolutionary struggle by working people the world over. $10. Also in Spanish, French, and Arabic.

Che Guevara Talks to Young People
The Argentine-born revolutionary leader challenges youth of Cuba and the world to study, to work, to become disciplined. To join the front lines of struggles, small and large. To politicize themselves and the work of their organizations. To become a different kind of human being as they strive with working people of all lands to transform the world. Eight talks from 1959 to 1964. $15. Also in Spanish.

www.pathfinderpress.com

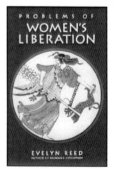

Malcolm X Talks to Young People

"You're living at a time of revolution," Malcolm told young people in the United Kingdom in December 1964. "And I for one will join in with anyone, I don't care what color you are, as long as you want to change the miserable condition that exists on this earth." Four talks and an interview given to young people in Ghana, the UK, and the United States in the last months of Malcolm's life. $15. Also in Spanish and French.

The Communist Manifesto

KARL MARX AND FREDERICK ENGELS

Why communism is not a set of preconceived principles but the line of march of the working class toward power, "springing from an existing class struggle, a historical movement going on under our very eyes." The founding document of the modern revolutionary workers movement. $5. Also in Spanish, French, and Arabic.

The Jewish Question
A Marxist Interpretation
ABRAM LEON

Traces the historical rationalizations of anti-Semitism to the fact that, in the centuries preceding the domination of industrial capitalism, Jews emerged as a "people-class" of merchants, moneylenders, and traders. Leon explains why the propertied rulers incite renewed Jew-hatred in the epoch of capitalism's decline. $25

PATHFINDER AROUND THE WORLD

Visit our website for a complete list of titles and to place orders

www.pathfinderpress.com

PATHFINDER DISTRIBUTORS

UNITED STATES
(and Caribbean, Latin America, and East Asia)

> Pathfinder Books, 306 W. 37th St., 13th Floor
> New York, NY 10018

CANADA

> Pathfinder Books, 7107 St. Denis, Suite 204
> Montreal, QC H2S 2S5

UNITED KINGDOM
(and Europe, Africa, Middle East, and South Asia)

> Pathfinder Books, 2nd Floor, 83 Kingsland High Street
> Dalston, London, E8 2PB

AUSTRALIA
(and Southeast Asia and the Pacific)

> Pathfinder, Level 1, 3/281–287 Beamish St., Campsie, NSW 2194
> Postal address: P.O. Box 164, Campsie, NSW 2194

NEW ZEALAND

> Pathfinder, 188a Onehunga Mall, Onehunga, Auckland 1061
> Postal address: P.O. Box 3025, Auckland 1140

Join the Pathfinder Readers Club
to get 15% discounts on all Pathfinder
titles and bigger discounts
on special offers.
Sign up at www.pathfinderpress.com
or through the distributors above.